America's
Founders

Other Books in the History Makers Series:

*History*MAKERS

America's Founders

By Michael V. Uschan

Lucent Books
P.O. Box 289011, San Diego, CA 92198-9011

In memory of Jay G. Sykes,
the journalism teacher who made me believe in myself,
both as a writer and as a person.

Library of Congress Cataloging-in-Publication Data

Uschan, Michael V., 1948–
  America's founders / by Michael V. Uschan.
    p.   cm. — (History makers)
  Includes bibliographical references and index.
  Summary: Discusses the influence of five well-known men—George
Washington, Benjamin Franklin, Thomas Jefferson, Alexander Hamilton,
and John Adams—on the early history of the United States.
  ISBN 1-56006-571-0 (lib. bdg. : alk. paper)
  1. Statesmen—United States—Biography—Juvenile literature.
2. Presidents—United States—Biography Juvenile literature. 3. United
States—History—Revolution, 1775–1783 Juvenile literature. 4. United
States—History—1783–1815 Juvenile literature. [1. United States—
History—Revolution, 1775–1783. 2. United States—History—
1783–1815. 3. Statesmen. 4. Presidents.] I. Title. II. Series.
E302.5.U84   2000
973.4'09'9—dc21   99-27390
[B]   CIP
                                                                   AC

Cover: (center) George Washington; (clockwise from top right) Benjamin
Franklin, Thomas Jefferson, John Adams, Alexander Hamilton

CONTENTS

FOREWORD

The literary form most often referred to as "multiple biography" was perfected in the first century A.D. by Plutarch, a perceptive and talented moralist and historian who hailed from the small town of Chaeronea in central Greece. His most famous work, *Parallel Lives*, consists of a long series of biographies of noteworthy ancient Greek and Roman statesmen and military leaders. Frequently, Plutarch compares a famous Greek to a famous Roman, pointing out similarities in personality and achievements. These expertly constructed and very readable tracts provided later historians and others, including playwrights like Shakespeare, with priceless information about prominent ancient personages and also inspired new generations of writers to tackle the multiple biography genre.

The Lucent History Makers series proudly carries on the venerable tradition handed down from Plutarch. Each volume in the series consists of a set of five to eight biographies of important and influential historical figures who were linked together by a common factor. In *Rulers of Ancient Rome*, for example, all the figures were generals, consuls, or emperors of either the Roman Republic or Empire; while the subjects of *Fighters Against American Slavery*, though they lived in different places and times, all shared the same goal, namely the eradication of human servitude. Mindful that politicians and military leaders are not (and never have been) the only people who shape the course of history, the editors of the series have also included representatives from a wide range of endeavors, including scientists, artists, writers, philosophers, religious leaders, and sports figures.

Each book is intended to give a range of figures—some well known, others less known; some who made a great impact on history, others who made only a small impact. For instance, by making Columbus's initial voyage possible, Spain's Queen Isabella I, featured in *Women Leaders of Nations*, helped to open up the New World to exploration and exploitation by the European powers. Unarguably, therefore, she made a major contribution to a series of events that had momentous consequences for the entire world. By contrast, Catherine II, the eighteenth-century Russian queen, and Golda Meir, the modern Israeli prime minister, did not play roles of global impact; however, their policies and actions significantly influenced the historical development of both their own countries and their regional neighbors. Regardless of their relative importance in the greater historical scheme, all of the figures chronicled in the History Makers series made contributions to posterity; and their public achievements, as well as what is known about their private lives, are presented and evaluated in light of the most recent scholarship.

In addition, each volume in the series is documented and substantiated by a wide array of primary and secondary source quotations. The primary source quotes enliven the text by presenting eyewitness views of the times and culture in which each history maker lived; while the secondary source quotes, taken from the works of respected modern scholars, offer expert elaboration and/or critical commentary. Each quote is footnoted, demonstrating to the reader exactly where biographers find their information. The footnotes also provide the reader with the means of conducting additional research. Finally, to further guide and illuminate readers, each volume in the series features photographs, two bibliographies, and a comprehensive index.

The History Makers series provides both students engaged in research and more casual readers with informative, enlightening, and entertaining overviews of individuals from a variety of circumstances, professions, and backgrounds. No doubt all of them, whether loved or hated, benevolent or cruel, constructive or destructive, will remain endlessly fascinating to each new generation seeking to identify the forces that shaped their world.

Five Who Changed History

Michel-Guillaume-Jean de Crèvecoeur, who was born in France but immigrated to America in 1759 and settled in Orange County, New York, wrote a book in 1782 called *Letters from an American Farmer*. Crèvecoeur explained what life was like in his new home-land and how the New World shaped its inhabitants, transforming them from loyal, devoted subjects of Great Britain, their mother country, into independent, defiant men and women who forged the American Revolution. In an essay titled "What Is an American," Crèvecoeur captured the essence of these newly minted Americans, these audacious colonials who dared challenge the world's strongest nation for their independence:

> He is an American who leaves behind him all his ancient prejudices and manners, receives new ones from the new mode of life he has embraced, the new government he obeys, and the new rank he holds. He becomes an American by being received in the broad lap of our great Alma Mater. Here individuals of all nations are melted into a new race of men, whose labours and posterity will one day cause great changes in the world. The American is a new man, who acts upon new principles; he must therefore entertain new ideas and form new opinions. This is an American.[1]

America's founders all fit Crèvecoeur's definition. Although none completely abandoned the "ancient prejudices and manners" of their former homelands, all adopted new principles, ideas, and opinions that inspired them to shatter the bonds holding them under the sway of Great Britain and to forge a new government, one that respected and protected the rights of individuals more than any other in history.

The Nation's Birth

From Crispus Attucks, the black dockworker who was killed along with four others in the 1770 Boston Massacre, to the 25,324 soldiers who died between 1775 and 1783, the American Revolution produced a multitude of heroes and heroines. The founders profiled here are the individuals who had the greatest impact on the birth of the United States.

Known simply as "the Father of His Country," George Washington, as commander of the Continental army, forged a military victory over the British. Called to politics after the war as America struggled to govern itself, Washington left his beloved Mount Vernon to preside over the Constitutional Convention and to help create the strong central government that he believed was necessary for the nation's survival. As its first president, Washington unified the nation and established the power and prestige of the office for all time.

Benjamin Franklin, a brilliant intellect who succeeded in many fields, represents the American success story: the individual who through talent and hard work betters himself socially and economically. One of thirteen children of a soap and candle maker, the self-educated Franklin became a wealthy businessman, noted publisher and author, and world-renowned scientist. Franklin played a major part in the intellectual battle that set the nation on its path to independence and was a key figure in the diplomatic war that helped win the American Revolution.

George Washington gestures with his hand while addressing delegates to the Constitutional Convention in 1787.

Thomas Jefferson, the nation's third president, was a gifted philosopher, architect, farmer, musician, and naturalist. As the famed eloquent writer of the Declaration of Independence, Jefferson fought to uphold the rights of average people, the glorious founding principle of America's democratic system of government. As president he negotiated the Louisiana Purchase, thus ensuring future westward expansion.

Alexander Hamilton fought with distinction during the Revolutionary War and was the main author of the *Federalist*, a series of essays that defended the U.S. Constitution and helped secure its ratification. As America's first treasury secretary, Hamilton put the fledgling nation on the path to financial stability and created economic policies that still benefit the country today.

John Adams, the nation's first vice president and its second president, was one of the earliest advocates of independence. His championing of the rights of the people to govern themselves helped create the way of life Americans enjoy today. Adams believed so deeply in these rights that he even represented British soldiers who were charged in the Boston Massacre, arguing that they acted in self-defense when attacked.

An Honored Place in History

Historian Page Smith believes that these historical figures deserve an honored spot in history not only for their accomplishments but also because they were somehow able to capture the hearts and minds of Americans for all time:

> Historians do not bestow greatness, nor can they withdraw it. Greatness accrues to an individual because he seized upon some essential portion of the popular imagination. He need meet only a single requirement of his times, a requirement rising out of the deepest levels of the collective consciousness to insure his immortality. Thus Washington's greatness was, in large part, to be found in his rocklike enduringness, that of Adams in his intelligent industry, of Hamilton in his financial genius, of Jefferson in his ability to articulate the noble ideals of democracy.[2]

Franklin, too, meets this requirement. Although these five represent only a fraction of the heroic men and women who helped create a new nation, their contributions were vital to winning freedom from Great Britain and shaping the new United States of America.

CHAPTER 1

The American Revolution: Two Revolutions in One

Four years after the United States defeated Great Britain to win its independence, Dr. Benjamin Rush, surgeon general for the Continental army and a cosigner of the Declaration of Independence, wrote, "There is nothing more common than to confound the terms of the American Revolution with those of the late American War. The American War is over: but that is far from the case with the American Revolution. On the contrary, nothing but the first act of that great drama is closed."[3]

Rush, like others, knew that all the bloody battles, thousands of deaths, and severe hardships that Americans endured from 1775 to 1783 achieved only one thing: freedom from British rule. The thirteen former colonies now faced the more difficult task of keeping their fragile union alive and learning to govern themselves.

The battle over ideas and political philosophies, both before and after the war, is not as dramatic or easy to understand as the war itself. But John Adams, the nation's second president, believed this revolution of the mind and spirit, one fired by a thirst for individual freedom, "began as early as the first plantation"[4] the English started in the New World.

Early Colonization

The first people to set foot in North America some twenty thousand years ago were ancestors of modern Native Americans who migrated during the Ice Age over a land bridge that connected northeastern Asia and Alaska. By the year 1500, 1 to 2 million Native Americans lived in what is now the United States.

Although Norwegian explorer Leif Eriksson is believed to have journeyed to Newfoundland in about the year 1000, Christopher Columbus is credited with discovering America in 1492 when he voyaged from Spain to San Salvador while seeking a trade route to Asia. Even though Columbus incorrectly believed San Salvador was just off the coast of Asia, his voyage opened North and South America to colonization. Spanish explorer Juan Ponce de León landed in Florida in 1513, and Hernán Cortés, also from Spain, reached modern-day Santa Cruz, California, in 1536 after traveling by land from Mexico.

When the New World's wealth of resources and labor made Spain the first worldwide power, France and Great Britain began lusting after these new lands. Samuel de Champlain founded the first permanent French settlement in Quebec in 1608, and France extended its power into northern and central North America.

Great Britain, lagging behind at first in the race to conquer the New World, started its first viable colony in Jamestown, Virginia, on May 13, 1607. Five years later, Dutch settlers founded what would eventually be known as New York City. On December 21, 1620, the Pilgrims arrived at Plymouth, Massachusetts.

In Great Britain, the Pilgrims had been persecuted because they disagreed with the teachings of the Church of England, the country's official church. Their desire for individual freedom, the siren song that has always lured immigrants to America, was embodied in the Mayflower Compact. Realizing they must govern themselves, the Pilgrims agreed to

While prayers are said for their safe passage, Pilgrims depart for the New World in July 1620.

combine our selves together into a civill body politick; for our better ordering, & preservation; and by virtue hearof to enacte, constitute, and frame shuch just & equall lawes, ordinances, Acts, constitutions, & offices, from time to time, as shall be thought most [proper] and convenicnt for the generall good of the colonie.[5]

One year earlier in Virginia, a council of twenty-two representatives had met for the first time to make laws governing the fledgling colony. This self-government was a right the Virginians would jealously guard in the future.

These first Americans believed from the very start that political authority in their new home should reside in the will of the people, not in a government far away across the Atlantic Ocean.

Early Colonial Life

Life was brutally hard for early colonists. Although some six thousand people had moved to Virginia by 1624, the population at that time was only twelve hundred because almost five out of six colonists had either gone home, died from sickness, or been killed by Native Americans. Native American tribes had at first welcomed settlers, but the relationship quickly became adversarial, as the authors of *The Americans: The History of a People and a Nation* explain:

> In general, the Indians first received the colonists on their shores with great curiosity, then with warm friendliness. Time and again, entire settlements such as Jamestown and Plymouth were saved from starvation by the Algonquins. If they had wished, they could have killed the colonists or forced them to flee back to their boats and the sea. It was only after unmistakable signs of settlers intending to take over their land that the Indians became aroused to their danger. By then it was too late. Despite brief but bloody wars, the colonists had too many beachheads on the continent. They were backed up by seemingly unending supplies of people and material from Europe.[6]

The colonists came to be called Americans. The southern colonies developed an agrarian society with a few rich plantation owners and a large lower class of slaves, indentured servants, and small farmers. (Indentured servants were men and women who agreed to work contracts, usually about five years, to pay their passage to America.) The northern colonies, which concentrated on developing commercial activities such as shipping and manufacturing, enjoyed more prosperity and had a larger middle class.

By 1763 an estimated 2.5 million Europeans lived in America, most of them farmers. Beyond the well-populated coast lay only wilderness broken by tiny scattered settlements and small towns, most with only twenty to seventy families. The few big cities were concentrated mainly in the north. Philadelphia, with forty thousand inhabitants, was the largest city in the English-speaking world after London; meanwhile New York had a population of twenty thousand; Boston, sixteen thousand; Charleston, South Carolina, twelve thousand; and Newport, Rhode Island, eleven thousand.

The colonies shared a basic pattern of local government and general control by Great Britain based on English political and legal institutions. Each colony had representative legislatures, similar systems of local administration, and governors who executed local laws, appointed officials, proposed legislation, and could summon and dismiss colonial legislatures.

Mercantilism

From the 1500s to 1700s, Great Britain and other European nations colonized new lands under an economic concept known as mercantilism. These nations believed the sole purpose of colonies was to enrich their "mother countries" either through natural resources, such as gold and silver, or through commercial trade.

One of America's new riches was tobacco, a plant that made southern colonists financially secure when smoking became popular in Europe. Tobacco production in Virginia and other southern colonies skyrocketed from 2,500 pounds in 1616 to nearly 30 million pounds in the late seventeenth century. A single farmer working two or three acres could produce as much as 1,200 pounds of cured tobacco and make a profit of more than 200 percent.

Unknown until Spanish explorers brought it back from the West Indies, tobacco was not common in England until the time of Sir Walter Raleigh, who was introduced to it by Native Americans. Although smoking quickly became popular in the Old World, historians John A. Garraty and Robert A. McCaughey explain that smoking, known today to be addictive and to cause health problems, was considered unhealthy even when it first appeared in Europe. British officials, however, allowed the trade to continue because it was profitable:

The Thirteen Colonies
(and dates of first
permanent settlements)

NOVA SCOTIA

MAINE
(PART OF MASS.)

NEW HAMPSHIRE (1623)

MASSACHUSETTS (1620)

L. Ontario

Albany

Boston

NEW YORK
(1624)

Newport

RHODE ISLAND (1636)
CONNECTICUT (1633)

L. Erie

PENNSYLVANIA
(1643)

New York City

Philadelphia

NEW JERSEY (1660)

Reserved for the
Indians by
Proclamation of 1763

DELAWARE (1638)

MARYLAND (1634)

VIRGINIA
(1607)

Richmond

Jamestown

Atlantic Ocean

Proclamation Line

NORTH CAROLINA
(c. 1653)

SOUTH CAROLINA
(1670)

North
America

Colonies

Charleston

GEORGIA
(1733)

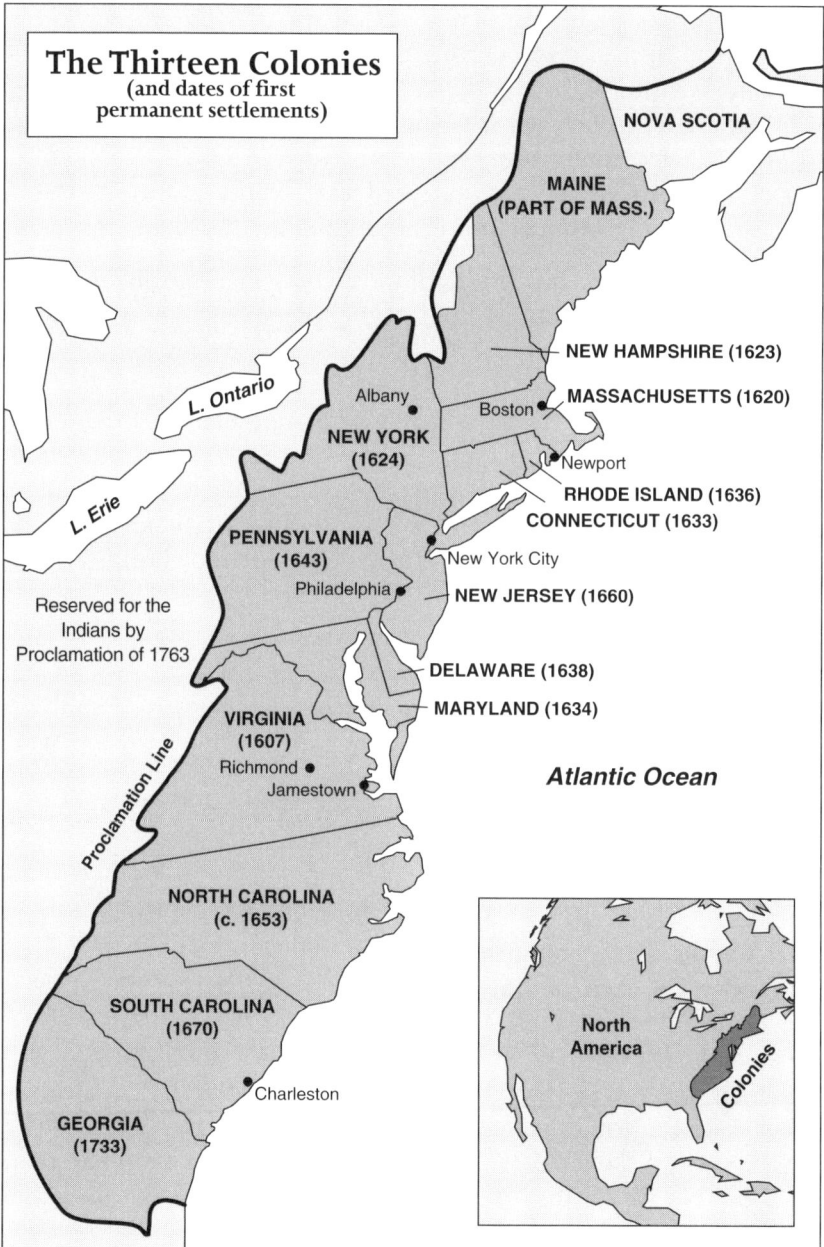

At first the London Company [the corporation that spon-
sored settlers in Virginia] discouraged its colonists from
growing tobacco. Since it clearly contained some habit-
forming drug, many people opposed its use. King James I
wrote a pamphlet attacking the weed, in which, among
other things, he anticipated the findings of modern cancer

researchers by saying that smoking was a "vile and stink-ing [habit] . . . dangerous to the Lungs." But English smokers and partakers of snuff ignored their king, and the Virginians ignored their company. By 1617 a pound of to-bacco was worth more than 5 shillings in London. Com-pany and Crown then changed their tune, granting the colonists a monopoly and encouraging them in every way.[7]

Although Americans also profited from growing tobacco, they could legally sell it only to English companies at fixed prices, en-abling British firms to make even more money by marketing it abroad. Americans also had to buy clothes, glass, books, and other products exclusively from Great Britain. This artificial eco-nomic relationship was legalized through the Navigation Acts of 1660 and 1663, which made the colonies economically dependent on their mother country. This one-way flow of riches to Great Britain would become an underlying cause for rebellion.

Early Calls for Union

During the seventeenth and eighteenth centuries, European na-tions were almost always at war. A major cause of the conflicts was competition for new colonies, which meant the wars were fought in both Europe and North America.

The French and Indian War, known in Europe as the Seven Years' War, began in 1754 when twenty-two-year-old George Washington and his small band of Virginia militia clashed in the Ohio Valley with a much larger force of French soldiers and Na-tive Americans. Washington had been sent there to halt the French buildup in the area. Although Washington was defeated on July 4, the engagement sparked a war that spread throughout the col-onies and Europe.

At the same time that Washington was under siege, delegates from several colonies were meeting in Albany, New York, to enlist the support of the Iroquois tribe against the French, who had their own Native American allies. The Iroquois rejected the plea, but out of the meeting came one of the first proposals to unify the colonies.

Benjamin Franklin proposed the Albany Plan of Union, which sought to unite the colonies so they could better defend and gov-ern themselves. Franklin suggested "that humble application be made for an act of Parliament of Great Britain by virtue of which one general government may be formed in America."[8] His plan in-cluded a president general to serve as chief executive and two leg-

George Washington leads a small band of soldiers on his mission to warn the French to leave the Ohio Valley. Their refusal to leave and an ensuing battle will ignite the French and Indian War.

islative houses composed of delegates from each of the colonies. Although the Albany Plan was rejected by both the colonies and Great Britain, Franklin succeeded in planting the idea of unification in the minds of Americans.

The French and Indian War ended in a humiliating defeat for France; under the terms of the 1763 Treaty of Paris, France abandoned all claims to North America except for two small islands near Newfoundland. Great Britain was ceded Canada and the eastern half of the Mississippi Valley from France and received Florida from Spain, France's military ally. Spain retained ownership of the port of New Orleans and of Louisiana, the area that included land drained by western tributaries of the Mississippi River.

"Half the continent," wrote historian Francis Parkman, "had changed hands at the scratch of a pen."[9] Ironically, this great English victory would lead to the American Revolution.

Taxation Without Representation

The war left Great Britain with a large debt and a huge new empire. Great Britain took a more active role in running the colonies, and it decided that Americans should help pay for the war since it

European Powers in North America, 1763

English

Spanish

NEWFOUND-LAND

Hudson Bay

Hudson's Bay Company

NOVA SCOTIA

Mississippi River

LOUISIANA

ENGLISH COLONIES

VIRGINIA

CAROLINAS

TEXAS

New Orleans

FLORIDA

Atlantic Ocean

Pacific Ocean

MEXICO

Gulf of Mexico

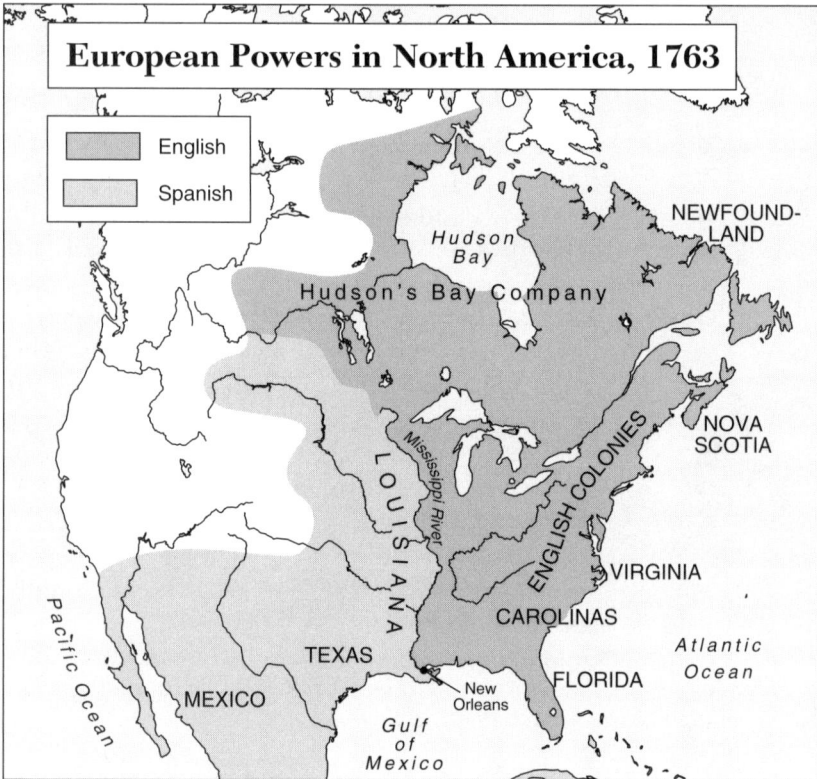

was fought to defend them. In 1764 Parliament, the British legislature, passed the Sugar Act to tax colonial imports including sugar, coffee, wine, and raw silk. The next year it enacted the Stamp Act, which taxed every kind of printed material from legal documents to playing cards.

Historian Page Smith claims the Stamp Act was more responsible for uniting the colonies than any other British action:

> The passage of the Stamp Act brought home to Americans of every colony and of every rank and condition their state of powerlessness and their dependence on [Great Britain]. This intolerable sense of subordination welded the people together, revealing that a remarkably heterogeneous collection of persons spread out over a vast extent of territory— and with, in many cases, very different origins, traditions, customs, and ideals—had become a people or, more properly, were capable of being almost instantly transformed into "a people." The evidence is in the rhetoric. In the space of a few weeks the colonists stopped talking of "our colony" or "our province" and began speaking of "our

poor degraded country" and of themselves as "Americans." For the first time a current of sympathy and mutual affection flowed from colony to colony.[10]

Delegates from nine colonies gathered in New York City in October 1765 as the Stamp Act Congress. They attacked it as "burthensome and grievous" and declared "it is unquestionably essential to the freedom of a people that no taxes be imposed on [the colonies] but with their own consent."[11]

The Sons of Liberty, informal groups of angry citizens, began harassing government officials who would issue the stamps. Their protests often turned violent as these "Liberty boys" looted and vandalized officials' homes and even tarred and feathered them, a painful process in which they were coated with hot tar and chicken feathers; some victims died from burns caused by the hot tar.

The colonies also began boycotting English products. The Daughters of Liberty quit buying tea, clothes, and other British goods and promised never to marry a man who bought English imports. These patriotic women distributed recipes for tea made from birch bark, sage, and rosemary and began weaving homespun cloth.

Colonists were so unified in their opposition to the tax that on November 1, 1765, the day the Stamp Act went into effect, not a single stamp was sold. The boycott crippled Britain's economy and forced officials to repeal the hated tax in March 1766.

But a joyous celebration was short-lived as Great Britain created new taxes and vowed to stamp out colonial dissent. In 1767 Parliament passed the Townshend Acts to tax lead, glass, tea, paint, and paper, and it began stricter enforcement of the Navigation

January...1770.

WILLIAM JACKSON,

an *IMPORTER*; at the

BRAZEN HEAD,

North Side of the TOWN-HOUSE,

and *Oppofite the Town-Pump, in*

Corn-hill, BOSTON.

It is defired that the SONS and DAUGHTERS of *LIBERTY*, would not buy any one thing of him, for in fo doing they will bring Difgrace upon *themfelves*, and their *Pofterity*, for *ever* and *ever*, AMEN.

The Sons and Daughters of Liberty in 1770 distributed handbills to persuade Boston residents to quit buying British imports.

Acts to stop products from being smuggled into and out of the colonies, which was robbing Great Britain of tax revenue.

The Townshend Acts were received no better than the Stamp Act. In their first year, the acts brought in only £295 since Americans once again refused to pay the taxes or buy taxable goods.

Although the Townshend Acts were a failure and lost money for Great Britain, which spent £17,000 to send soldiers to collect the taxes, King George III refused to change the policy.

George III, who had succeeded his grandfather as king at age twenty-two in 1760, became determined to bend the unruly colonists to his will. The king opened the 1769 session of Parliament by promising to defeat "the mischievous designs of those turbulent and seditious [rebels]" who had "deluded members of my subjects in America."[12]

Sons of Liberty

The Sons of Liberty was the name adopted by American colonists who began opposing British rule years before the Revolutionary War. Ironically, the name came from a member of Parliament, Irish-born Isaac Barre, who in 1765 opposed passage of the Stamp Act.

In Liberty! The American Revolution, *author Thomas Fleming describes Barre's fiery speech about Americans, who he came to know while fighting in the French and Indian War, in which he lost an eye in combat.*

"Charles Townshend—the playboy grandson of the Duke of Newcastle known as Champagne Charlie—argued that the colonies were spoiled brats if they would not want to pay the Stamp Act. 'And now will these Americans, children planted by our care, nourished up by our indulgence until they are grown to a degree of strength and opulence and protected by our arms, will they grudge to contribute their mite to relieve us from the heavy burden which we lie under?'

Barre then answered Townshend. 'They planted by your care! No! Your oppressions planted 'em in America. They fled your tyranny to a then uncultivated and inhospitable country—where they exposed themselves to the hardships to which human nature is liable, and among others to the cruelties of a savage foe. They nourished by your indulgence! They grew by your neglect of 'em. As soon as you began to care about 'em, that care was exercised by sending persons to rule over 'em . . . whose behavior on many occasions has caused the blood of these Sons of Liberty to recoil within them. . . . They protected by your arms! They have nobly taken up arms in your defense, have exerted a valour amidst their constant and laborious industry for the defence of a country whose frontier [is] drench'd in blood.'

Barre's eloquence failed to stop passage of the Stamp Act. But his words made him a hero in America and gave birth to one of the most famous nicknames in U.S. history."

Prelude to War

Residents of Boston, who were already leading the drive for independence, became even more militant in September 1768 when a thousand soldiers arrived in the port city to maintain control and collect taxes. Citizens and soldiers hated each other, and violent confrontations soon broke out.

The most serious occurred March 5, 1770, when an angry mob harassed British soldiers after one of the soldiers had struck a youth who taunted him. The soldiers fired into the crowd, killing five people. Known as the Boston Massacre, the incident outraged the public because it was the first time that soldiers had fired on Americans, marking an important milestone in the path toward revolution.

The Townshend Acts were repealed a month later, but in April 1773 Parliament, still determined to raise money from the colonies, passed the Tea Act. Even though taxed tea cost less than smuggled tea, colonists again believed their rights were being violated and the motto No Taxation Without Representation became their battle cry.

The culmination of a series of protests in Boston came December 16, 1773, after five thousand people met to speak out against the tax. As the gathering broke up, protesters soon heard the cries, "The Mohawks are come!" Some two hundred Sons of Liberty had arrived disguised as Native Americans. Draped in blankets, heads adorned with feathers and faces decorated with paint, they marched with a large crowd of onlookers to the docks, where they boarded three ships and dumped 342 chests of tea into the sea.

The Boston Tea Party, as it was called, was an insult King George III could not bear. "The die is now cast," he wrote. "The colonies must either submit or triumph."[13] Parliament responded in March 1774 by passing the Intolerable Acts, and the king chose Lieutenant General Thomas Gage to enforce them. In May he arrived in Boston with four thousand redcoats, the nickname given to British soldiers because of their traditional crimson uniforms.

Also called the Coercive Acts, the Intolerable Acts were designed to punish the colony of Massachusetts, make it pay for the tea, and stamp out rebellion by imposing martial law. The acts limited local government, closed Boston's port, named Gage the colony's governor, and imposed a new quartering act that allowed British troops to live in civilians' private homes.

These repressive measures inflamed the colonies, uniting them and pushing them toward revolution. When representatives of all

Sons of Liberty disguised as Native Americans toss chests of tea overboard to protest English taxes.

thirteen colonies, except Georgia, met in Philadelphia in September 1774 for the First Continental Congress, John Adams, a Massachusetts delegate, claimed Parliament had no right to dictate laws to the colonies: "The foundation . . . of all free government is a right [of] the people to participate in their legislative council."[14]

The Continental Congress condemned British actions toward the colonies and organized the Continental Association to ban all trade with Great Britain until the Intolerable Acts were repealed. The congress also endorsed a Massachusetts proposal to raise a standing army and agreed to meet again in May 1775.

But by then, the Revolutionary War had already begun.

The War for Independence Begins

On March 23, 1775, Patrick Henry, a member of the Virginia House of Burgesses who was one of the most fiery patriots demanding freedom, said war with Great Britain was inevitable. When Virginia lawmakers met at St. John's Church in Richmond in defiance of royal orders dissolving the legislative body, Henry claimed the king had decided to dominate the colonies through military force. "We must fight," Henry declared in one of the most famous speeches of the Revolution:

> Gentlemen may cry, peace! peace—but there is no peace. The war is actually begun! The next gale that sweeps from the North will bring to our ears the clash of resounding

Thomas Paine and Common Sense

Born in England in 1737, Thomas Paine had only been in America for two years when he wrote Common Sense, *a fifty-page pamphlet that helped persuade many Americans to join the fight for independence. Historian Page Smith believes that when Paine came to America in late 1774, he already had a revolutionary fervor born of his own unhappy life.*

"The time was ripe for a squinty-eyed English stay-maker [corset maker] with a large, pockmarked nose to occupy the center of the stage—Thomas Paine. He was a self educated, working class Englishman who had an impoverished and unhappy childhood. He could not believe that god had intended that the rich should grind down the poor; or, as Sir Algernon Sidney had put it, that some were born with saddles on their backs and others were born booted and spurred to ride them. *Common Sense* was written for the common man. It came out of Thomas Paine's own guts—out of the bitter years of poverty, the soured dreams."

The words Paine wrote in Common Sense *helped light the flame of revolution throughout America.*

"Everything that is right or reasonable calls for separation. The blood of the slain, the weeping voice of nature cries, '*Tis time to part.*' Even the distance at which the almighty hath placed England and America is a strong and natural proof that the authority of the one over the other was never the design of heaven."

He ended with an emotional, fiery plea to readers to join the revolution: "O ye that love mankind! Ye that dare oppose not only the tyranny but the tyrant, stand forth!"

Published in Philadelphia on January 9, 1776, the work sold more than 130,000 copies in just three months, but Paine remained poor because he refused to accept any royalties. He answered his own call to arms by joining the Continental army.

COMMON SENSE;

ADDRESSED TO THE

INHABITANTS

O F

A M E R I C A,

On the following interesting

S U B J E C T S.

I. Of the Origin and Design of Government in general, with concise Remarks on the English Constitution.

II. Of Monarchy and Hereditary Succession.

III. Thoughts on the present State of American Affairs.

IV. Of the present Ability of America, with some miscellaneous Reflections.

Man knows no Master save creating HEAVEN, Or those whom choice and common good ordain.

THOMSON.

PHILADELPHIA;

Printed, and Sold, by R. BELL, in Third-Street.

MDCCLXXVI.

Thomas Paine's dramatic call to arms in Common Sense *persuaded tens of thousands of colonists to join the fight for independence.*

arms. Is life so dear, or peace so sweet, as to be purchased at the price of chains and slavery? Forbid it, Almighty God! I know not what course others may take; but as for me, give me liberty or give me death![15]

Henry's speech was quite prophetic. The Revolutionary War began on April 19 when rebels battled British soldiers at Lexington and Concord, two small communities west of Boston. The redcoats were marching from Boston to Concord to destroy rebel arms. At dawn that day, the first of some seven hundred redcoats arrived in Lexington, five miles east of Concord. They were confronted there by about seventy minutemen, members of informal militia units that had been training to fight the British since the fall of 1774.

Captain John Pitcairn ordered the Americans to leave: "Ye villains, ye rebels disperse! Lay down your arms! Why don't ye lay down your arms?"[16] After a short argument, the minutemen did begin to leave. Suddenly a shot rang out; to this day no one knows which side fired first. British soldiers then unleashed a withering volley that killed eight minutemen. After marching to Concord, where the British discovered that most of the supplies had been removed to safety, they headed back to Boston.

Patrick Henry's stirring speech was one of the American Revolution's most moving pieces of oratory. His words have lived through the centuries, becoming a symbol for the fierce desire Americans have always had for freedom.

A Melting Pot Army

The minutemen, the Continental army, and various state militias that fought in the American Revolution included African Americans as well as soldiers from many countries. Some of the officers are well known such as the marquis de Lafayette of France, Thaddeus Kosciusko of Poland, and Baron Friedrich von Steuben of Germany. In George Washington: A Life, *historian Willard Sterne Randall notes that many more ethnic groups were represented in the war that established America's right to exist.*

"A history of the Revolution based on evidence would represent a rich ethnic tapestry, not an all-white, all WASP [white Anglo-Saxon Protestant] pantheon. Revolutionary politics and the ranks of revolutionary soldiers include Czechs, Poles, Hungarians, Greeks, Danes, Swedes, Italians, Bohemians, Dutch, Germans, Scots, Irish, Swiss, French, Africans, Indians, Protestants, Catholics, and Jews from many countries. The British army in America was preponderantly made up of Irish, Scottish, and German mercenaries, more Germans fighting on the English side than Englishmen.

In virtually every military engagement, what today would be called ethnic Americans took part. Polish American sailors in the crew of the American ship *Bonhomme Richard* fought under a famous Scottish American Captain, John Paul Jones. Two regiments of Italians recruited in their homeland fought under the French flag at Yorktown, while their countryman, Filippo Mazzei, Thomas Jefferson's next-door neighbor in Virginia, took a musket and marched off as a private in 1887. North and South, blacks fought on both sides, both sides offering freedom if they survived. An estimated 6,500 blacks fought under Washington, more than double that number on the British [side]. And all through the war, Jewish Americans fought, suffered, and gave often all they had to keep the Revolution and its army and navies alive."

Minutemen from surrounding towns and villages poured into the area and attacked the retreating redcoats, firing on them from behind trees and stone walls. Gage was forced to send 1,500 more soldiers to rescue his initial force, and by day's end the British suffered 273 dead or wounded while the Americans had fewer than 100 casualties. The colonists had proved they could stand up to the vaunted British army.

The Revolutionary War

Gage once said, "It is impossible to beat the notion of liberty out of these people. It is rooted in 'em from childhood."[17] This overwhelming desire for freedom fueled the American spirit during the war.

On May 10, 1775, the Second Continental Congress convened in Philadelphia. During this two-month-long meeting, delegates established the Continental Congress as the central government for the "United Colonies of America," designated troops fighting near Boston the Continental army, and named George Washington commander in chief. Although the war had actually begun, the Continental Congress, over the protest of Adams and some other delegates, offered the Olive Branch petition to King George III. The petition affirmed American loyalty to the monarch and asked him to end Parliament's policies toward the colonies. King George rejected it.

One of the legendary battles of the American Revolution occurred before Washington could get to Boston. The Battle of Bunker Hill, already under way while Congress met, pitted rebel forces against eight thousand British troops for control of Bunker Hill and Breed's Hill in Charlestown, a peninsula north of Boston across the Charles River.

Although the British were victorious by June 17, the feisty, ill-equipped Americans made them pay dearly, killing more than one thousand redcoats out of a force of some twenty-five hundred while losing only four hundred men themselves. One English report said that "never had the British army so ungenerous an enemy to oppose" because the Americans concealed themselves behind trees and fortifications, shot at them, and then retreated. "What an unfair method of carrying on a war!"[18] it declared. The colonists had learned the unorthodox tactics during fights with Native Americans.

Many historians consider America's victory over the most powerful land and naval force of the time miraculous. Major contributing factors were aid from France starting in 1778, long supply lines, problems in communication between British officers and faraway superiors, and poor British military and civilian leadership.

Historian Thomas Fleming, however, credits Washington's military strategy with winning the war:

> In seven years he won only three clear cut victories—Trenton, Princeton, and Yorktown—and in seven others was defeated or at best could claim a draw. But he won by devising a superior strategy. After defeat on Long Island in 1776, he realized the British had a bigger, better-trained army and a huge [navy]. While everyone else wrung their hands and lamented that the war was lost, Washington

kept his head and devised a new strategy. Henceforth, he wrote to Congress, the war would be "defensive." Americans would "avoid a general action" and never put "anything to the risque." Instead they would "protract the war." Lieutenant General David Richard Palmer, the former

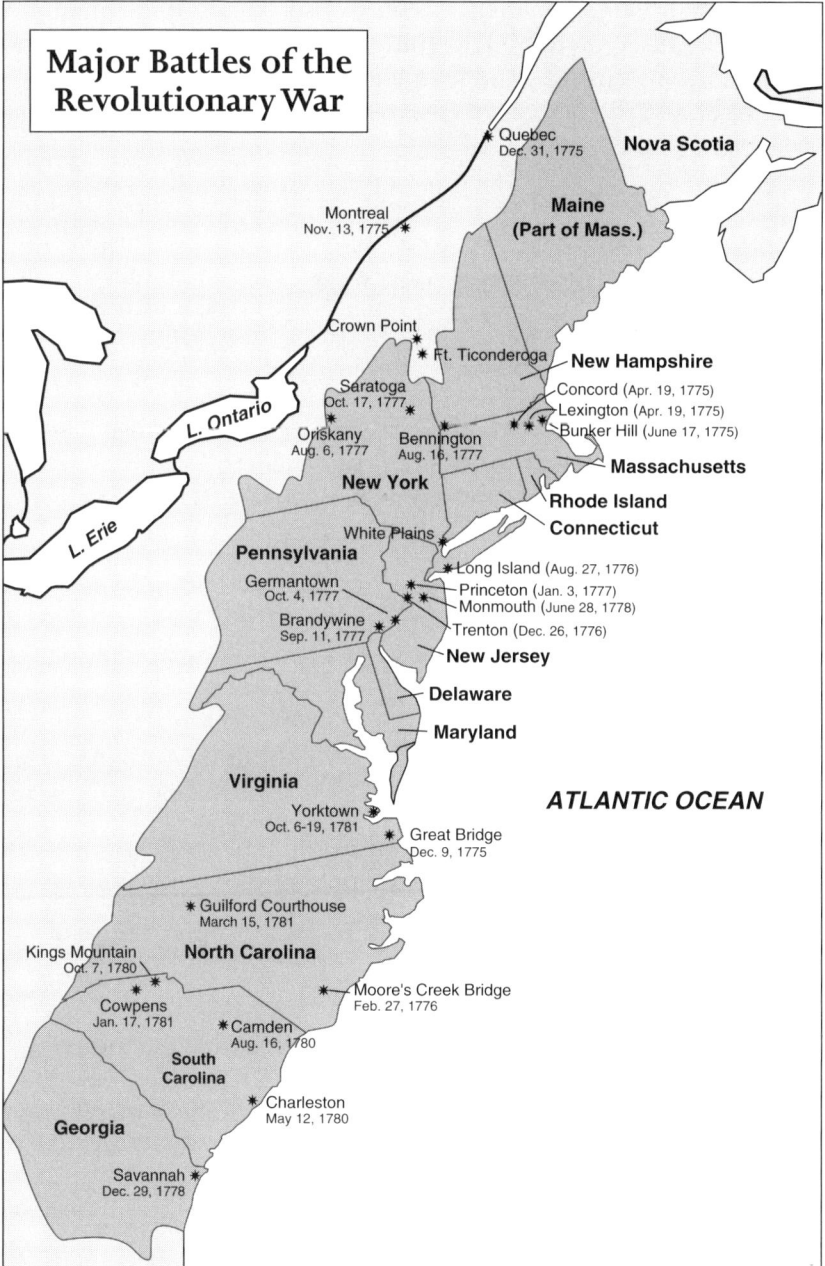

Major Battles of the Revolutionary War

Quebec
Dec. 31, 1775

Nova Scotia

Montreal
Nov. 13, 1775

Maine
(Part of Mass.)

Crown Point

Ft. Ticonderoga

New Hampshire

Saratoga
Oct. 17, 1777

Concord (Apr. 19, 1775)
Lexington (Apr. 19, 1775)
Bunker Hill (June 17, 1775)

Oriskany
Aug. 6, 1777

Bennington
Aug. 16, 1777

Massachusetts

New York

Rhode Island

L. Ontario

White Plains

Connecticut

L. Erie

Pennsylvania

Long Island (Aug. 27, 1776)

Germantown
Oct. 4, 1777

Princeton (Jan. 3, 1777)
Monmouth (June 28, 1778)

Brandywine
Sep. 11, 1777

Trenton (Dec. 26, 1776)

New Jersey

Delaware

Maryland

Virginia

ATLANTIC OCEAN

Yorktown
Oct. 6-19, 1781

Great Bridge
Dec. 9, 1775

Guilford Courthouse
March 15, 1781

Kings Mountain
Oct. 7, 1780

North Carolina

Cowpens
Jan. 17, 1781

Moore's Creek Bridge
Feb. 27, 1776

Camden
Aug. 16, 1780

South
Carolina

Charleston
May 12, 1780

Georgia

Savannah
Dec. 29, 1778

Superintendent of West Point, has called this letter "a masterpiece of strategic thought, a brilliant blueprint permitting a weak force to combat a powerful opponent." While the British army floundered after the Continental Army, vainly pursuing a general action, Washington retreated or remained on the defensive and struck when and where the British least expected him. Slowly but surely, the British Parliament grew weary of this seemingly unwinnable war. Washington's victory at Yorktown thus became the knockout blow.[19]

The end came October 19, 1781, after a month-long siege of British troops at Yorktown, Virginia, with the surrender of Lord Charles Cornwallis, who was outnumbered two-to-one by nine thousand American and eight thousand French soldiers. When British prime minister Lord Frederick North heard of the surrender, he turned pale and said, "O God! it is all over!"[20]

America, however, would find it easier to win a war than to learn to govern itself.

Creating a New Form of Government

Years later John Adams would ask, "What do we mean by the Revolution. The War? That was no part of the Revolution. It was only an effect and consequence of it. The Revolution was in the minds of the people, and this was effected, from 1760 to 1775, in the course of fifteen years before a drop of blood was drawn at Lexington."[21]

Like Benjamin Rush, Adams believed that the real Revolution was the one that changed how people felt about the way they lived and were governed. The real victory was the freedom Americans now had to govern themselves. But after the Treaty of Paris officially ended the war in 1783 the fledgling nation fell into an economic depression, colonies began bickering over unsettled western lands, and the fragile bonds uniting the states appeared ready to break.

The states had taken the first step toward creating a new government in May 1776 when delegates to the Second Continental Congress in Philadelphia decided to compose the Declaration of Independence. They entrusted the writing to Thomas Jefferson, a young Virginia planter who produced a masterpiece of political thought. Adopted July 4, it boldly declared:

> We hold these truths to be self-evident, that all men are created equal, that they are endowed by their Creator with

Delegates to the Second Continental Congress line up to sign the Declaration of Independence. The document was approved July 4 but members of Congress did not sign it until August 2.

certain unalienable Rights, that among these are Life, Liberty and the pursuit of Happiness. That to secure these rights, Governments are instituted among Men, deriving their just powers from the consent of the governed. That whenever any Form of Government becomes destructive of these ends, it is the Right of the People to alter or to abolish it, and to institute new Government, laying its foundation on such principles and organizing its powers in such form, as to them shall seem most likely to effect their Safety and Happiness.[22]

Considering that at the time all other nations were monarchies, this philosophy was a bold step forward in giving citizens freedom and equality, but creating a government based on such ideals was difficult. The Continental Congress had trouble governing from the beginning because it had little power to make the states cooperate and obey laws.

Even after the states approved the Articles of Confederation in 1781, which formalized this relationship, the new central government did not have power to adequately govern. The confederation's most serious flaw was that it denied the new government the right to raise taxes, denying it the funds to properly govern the new nation.

Washington, who had retired to his Virginia plantation, was one of the leaders worried about the fate of his nation. "The consequences," he wrote, "of . . . [an] inefficient government are too obvious to be dwelt upon. Thirteen sovereignties pulling against each other, and all tugging at the federal head, will soon bring ruin upon the whole. Let us have [government] by which our lives, liberty, and property will be secured, or let us know the worst at once."[23]

Washington and other prominent leaders called for a meeting in Philadelphia in 1787 to revise the Articles of Confederation. Instead, delegates scrapped the articles and drafted an entirely new document, the Constitution. It was approved by delegates September 17, and when the colonies ratified it the following year, it became the law of the land.

The Constitution gave the federal government new powers and created the system of government Americans know today: a president who is chief executive; two houses of Congress, the Senate and the House of Representatives; a judicial branch including the Supreme Court; and a series of checks and balances so none of the three branches of government—executive, legislative, and judicial— would have too much power. More importantly, it affirmed basic individual rights for Americans.

"A New Age Now Begins"

Historian Page Smith states that the American Revolution allowed the creation of "a new age, a new human order, in which no man was sentenced by the chance of birth to subordination and exploitation and no class of men was ordained to rule over others. These were America's Revolutionary credentials—a new dispensation for the human race, a new hope for humanity."[24]

On the reverse side of the Great Seal of the United States is a phrase from the Roman poet Virgil: *"Novus Ordo Seclorum."* The Latin words mean "a new age now begins."

And so it had for the United States of America.

CHAPTER 2

George Washington: Father of His Country

George Washington did many things, but he never tossed a dollar across the Potomac River or chopped down a cherry tree. The difficulty in understanding this complex man is that Washington, more than any other founder, has been draped in myth and idolized by Americans since the nation's birth.

In a biography for children written after Washington's death in 1799, Parson Mason Weems manufactured legends that some people today still believe are true. Weems claims that when Washington was about six years old he was made "the wealthy master of a hatchet" and damaged a cherry tree. When his father asked George if he had "killed that beautiful little cherry tree yonder in the garden?" the future president responded, "I can't tell a lie, Pa; you know I can't tell a lie. I did cut it with my hatchet."[25]

Historians John A. Garraty and Robert A. McCaughey write that Washington's strength of character, such as his unrelenting honesty symbolized by this tall tale, is what made him an endearing symbol to most Americans:

> Stern, cold, a man of few words, the great Virginian did not seem a likely candidate for hero worship. "My countenance never yet revealed my feelings," he himself admitted. Yet he had qualities that made people name babies after him and call him "the Father of His Country" long before the war was won. People of all sections, from every walk of life, looked on Washington as the embodiment of American virtues: a man of deed rather than words; a man of substance accustomed to luxury yet capable of enduring great hardship stoically and as much at home in the wilderness as an Indian; a bold Patriot, quick to take arms against British tyranny, yet eminently respectable. The Revolution might have been won without Washington, but it is unlikely that the free United States would have become so easily a true nation had he not been at its call."[26]

Youth and Education

Washington was born on February 22, 1732, in Westmoreland County, Virginia, to Augustine Washington, a planter, and Mary Ball Washington. Washington's father died in 1743, when young George was only eleven years old. Washington, who was never close to his strict mother, began spending most of his time with Lawrence Washington, an older half brother from his father's first marriage. Lawrence lived at Mount Vernon, the plantation he inherited when their father died. After assuming the plantation, Lawrence changed its name from Epsewasson to Mount Vernon to honor British admiral Edward Vernon, his commanding officer in the navy.

Raised on Ferry Farm, the plantation on the Rappahannock River that he would inherit at age twenty-one, Washington never had much formal education, something he always regretted. "I conceive," he once said, "a knowledge of books is the basis upon which other knowledge is to be built."[27] He studied geography, military history, agriculture, mathematics, and surveying at home with tutors and at a small school.

George Washington began working as a surveyor at age sixteen. The job allowed the teenager to travel, earn his own money, and become independent of his mother.

Washington trained to be a surveyor, and in 1748, at age sixteen, he was hired as an assistant for a group that traveled across the Blue Ridge Mountains to map land owned by an English lord. Biographer Willard Sterne Randall writes that the trip was one of the pivotal events in Washington's life: "It marked his virtual independence from his mother—once he had cash in his pocket from surveying, there were fewer occasions when he had to go to her and ask. He began doing more surveying. He bought fashionable clothes, bought a sword and took fencing lessons, dancing lessons, and was now considered a man rather than a boy."[28]

When Washington turned twenty-one in 1753, he inherited the 224-acre Ferry Farm, ten slaves, and nearly 2,300 acres of land. He also owned 2,000 acres in the Shenandoah Valley purchased with his earnings as a surveyor. That same month he was named a major in the Virginia militia. His brother Lawrence's service in the British navy had led Washington to seek a military career; his wealth and standing made the commission possible.

The French and Indian War

For nearly a century the English and French had contested ownership of the Appalachian region from the Great Lakes south to the Ohio River and west to the Mississippi River. In December 1753, Virginia's Governor Robert Dinwiddie sent Washington to Fort Le Bouef (Buffalo), ten miles south of Lake Erie, to tell the French they were intruding on English territory.

When Washington returned after the French ignored his warning, Dinwiddie promoted Washington to lieutenant colonel. On April 16, 1754, Dinwiddie sent Washington back with three hundred soldiers to forcefully remove the French. On May 28 Washington's force attacked a French scouting party, killing ten people and taking twenty-one prisoners. In the bravado of youth, Washington describes his first trial by combat: "I heard the bullets whistle, and believe me there is something charming in the sound."[29]

Fearing a counter attack, Washington ordered his men to build Fort Necessity, a crude stockade of felled trees near present-day Uniontown, Pennsylvania. On July 3, one thousand members of a combined French and Native American force surrounded the fort and, in Washington's words, "from every little rising, tree, stump, stone and bush, kept up a constant, galling fire upon us."[30] Because more than one hundred of his men were killed or wounded in the nine-hour battle and many more were too ill to fight, Washington surrendered on July 4.

Washington's Rules to Live By

In George Washington: A Life, *Willard Sterne Randall claims that Washington's strong moral character, which more than anything else made him a heroic figure to Americans, was greatly shaped by 110 "Rules of Civility and Decent Behavior" that he copied by hand into notebooks when he was a youngster. The rules covered everything from morality to table manners.*

"*Rule 1:* Every action done in company ought to be done with some sign of respect to those that are present. *Rule 5:* If you cough, sneeze, sigh or yawn, do it not loud but privately. *Rule 9:* Spit not in the fire. *Rule 11:* Shift not yourself in the sight of others nor gnaw your nails. *Rule 19:* Let your countenance be pleasant but, in serious matters, somewhat grave. *Rule 22:* Show not yourself glad at the misfortune of another, though he were your enemy. *Rule 40:* Strive not with your superiors in argument, but always submit your judgment to others with modesty. *Rule 56:* Associate yourself with men of good quality if you esteem your own reputation, for 'tis better to be alone than in bad company. *Rule 73:* Think before you speak. Pronounce not imperfectly nor bring out your words too hastily but orderly and distinctly."

Written by French Jesuit priests, Washington considered the rules his gospel, as Randall elaborates.

"There were limits to what George could learn by observation and he already was developing a fondness for rules and order. His father had been away most of the time; his mother placed little value on order. How else was he to learn except by book? Washington practiced these rules more closely than the precepts of any religion. In the absence of a father and in contention with his mother, he espoused them as dogma, and his personal code of conduct closely paralleled them."

When Washington's confrontation ignited the French and Indian War, Great Britain sent Major General Edward Braddock to America with twenty-one hundred soldiers. Desiring to learn more about the art of war, Washington became an aide to Braddock and accompanied him on a retaliatory mission to Fort Duquesne, located near present-day Pittsburgh. The French attacked July 9 in the Battle of Monongahela, killing Braddock and more than a thousand soldiers in a bloody English defeat.

Washington escaped unharmed, but the battle changed his romantic notion of gaily whistling bullets. "I had four bullets through my coat and two horses shot under me,"[31] he wrote his mother. In a letter to a friend he recounted the British retreat: "The shocking scenes are not to be described. The dead, the dying, the groans, lamentations and cries along the road of the wounded for help were enough to pierce a heart of [stone]."[32]

Mount Vernon and Love

After two years of war, Washington rode home to Mount Vernon in the late summer of 1755. Lawrence had died in 1752, and Washington had agreed to rent Mount Vernon from his sister-in-law for fifteen thousand pounds of tobacco annually. Because Lawrence and his wife had no children, Washington would inherit Mount Vernon when his sister-in-law died.

Washington loved overseeing the plantation and spent many hours riding his land, supervising and directing its daily work. One of the first to realize that planting tobacco constantly in one field would ruin the soil, Washington began growing other crops and used fertilizer to increase crop production.

Still fascinated by military life, Washington continued to serve as commander in chief of a one-thousand-man Virginia army that fought marauding Native Americans. During one such campaign in the fall of 1757, his chronic dysentery flared up and he went home to recover.

Although generally healthy, Washington was plagued by occasional bouts of dysentery and malaria. In 1751, while on a trip to Barbados with Lawrence, he had contracted smallpox, which left his face permanently scarred. Suffering in 1757 from pyorrhea, a gum disease, he allowed his teeth to be pulled and wore false teeth the rest of his life. Because dentures then were crude and uncomfortable, Washington rarely smiled, making him look grim in portraits.

Mount Vernon, the plantation George Washington loved so deeply. He was always happiest when he was at home, tending to Mount Vernon's simple, everyday activities.

On January 6, 1759, after a courtship of several months, Washington married Martha Dandridge Custis, the richest widow in Virginia after inheriting 17,438 acres and a large sum of money from her late husband. She had two children, John and Martha, but the Washingtons had no children together. Because Washington was ill

Washington Portrait

You need only look at a dollar bill to see what George Washington looked like. But that portrait cannot convey the imposing physical presence generated by Washington, who towered over most men of his time and was very strong.

But in The War for Independence: The Story of the American Revolution, *Albert Marrin maintains that Washington's "real strengths were not physical but moral. Thomas Jefferson, who knew him well, described him as 'a wise, a good, and a great man.' He had a keen sense of responsibility and devotion to duty. No man cared more for the soldiers' welfare than the commander in chief." Marrin offers insight into Washington's physical appearance.*

"He stood [over] six feet tall and weighed over two hundred pounds. Broad-shouldered, he had long arms and legs, and enormous hands. Yet, despite his size, he moved gracefully. A natural in the saddle, he was said to be the finest horseman in America. Washington wasn't handsome. He had a large red nose, gray-blue eyes, and a face pitted with smallpox scars. His voice was sometimes difficult to understand because of his teeth, which were false.

Although otherwise healthy, poor teeth made him miserable all his adult life. He had countless pairs of dentures made from wood, hippopotamus ivory, and the teeth of humans, cows, pigs, and elk. One pair of false teeth was set in lead, weighed three pounds, and was connected with heavy steel springs. No wonder he seldom smiled."

In portraits, George Washington always appears grim and unsmiling. He never smiled because the false teeth he wore were uncomfortable.

again after another military expedition, the dimunitive Martha, who was less than five feet tall, spent the first six months of their marriage nursing him back to health.

Commander in Chief

On his twenty-seventh birthday in 1759, Washington began his fifteen-year career in the Virginia House of Burgesses. Although originally loyal to England, Washington came to resent British colonial interference, particularly taxes that hurt him financially. By the time of the Stamp Act, Washington had written, "At a time when our lordly masters in Great Britain will be satisfied with nothing less than the deprivation of American freedom, it seems highly necessary that something should be done to maintain the liberty which we have derived from our ancestors."[33]

Diminutive Martha Washington was the great love of George Washington's life. She even spent winters with him during the Revolutionary War.

Washington, along with fellow Virginians Thomas Jefferson and Patrick Henry, advocated independence. At the First Continental Congress in 1774, he supported a declaration of rights for the colonies. When Washington wore his uniform to the opening sessions of the Second Continental Congress, some delegates complained he was campaigning for the job of military commander; he said he wore it simply to show that the time for reconciliation was over. Nonetheless, on June 15, 1775, Congress unanimously elected Washington to head the new Continental army, an honor he humbly accepted.

"I will enter upon the momentous duty and exert every power I possess for support of the glorious cause," Washington said. "But I beg it may be remembered by every gentleman in the room, that I this day declare with the utmost sincerity, I do not think myself equal to the command I am honored with."[34]

The Revolutionary War

When Washington took command of the fifteen-thousand-man Continental army in Boston on July 2, he knew his soldiers were brave; they had already stood up to the British at Bunker Hill. Historian Albert Marrin describes how they beat back the initial British charge:

> The Redcoats started advancing, like a bright red carpet being unrolled, marching in silence to the tap-tap of drums to set the marching pace. Old Put [Israel Putnam] told the Americans, "Don't fire until you see the whites of their eyes, then fire low." [The British] got closer and closer

until their faces were visible. Then they obeyed Old Put. A hail of lead shredded their ranks but they kept coming again and again until, finally, they broke.[35]

The courageous rebels eventually retreated when they ran out of ammunition. A lack of supplies and inadequate funds from Congress plagued Washington throughout the war. Late in 1780 he wrote: "We have been half of our time without provision, and are likely to continue so. We have no [supplies of gunpowder or arms], nor money to form them, and in a little time we shall have no men, if we had money to pay them. We have lived upon [promises] 'till we can live no longer. The history of the war is a history of false hopes."[36]

Facing a superior force and limited supplies, Washington devised a tactic of hit-and-run attacks, the greatest of which came on Christmas night 1776. By December the English, who that summer and fall had pushed the Continental army out of New York and across the Delaware River into Pennsylvania, had settled into winter quarters in New Jersey.

Although Washington's troops were poorly clothed—many had to wrap scarves around their bare feet because they had no shoes—at 11 P.M. on December 25, Washington led his army across the Delaware River during a blinding snowstorm. His army then marched nine miles to Trenton, New Jersey, and at 8 A.M. surprised a unit of Hessians, German mercenaries hired to fight for the British, who were sleeping off a raucous Christmas celebration. The Americans killed 22 enemy soldiers, wounded 85, took 918 prisoners, and seized badly needed supplies. Only two Americans were wounded. As historian Page Smith writes,

> Perhaps the most important [factor in the victory] was simply Washington's physical stamina. Where an ordinary man would have long since come to the end of his rope both emotionally and physically, Washington was still in command of himself and of his army. In terms of endurance, it was one of the most remarkable performances by a general in all military history. By an act of his will, he drove a pathetic remnant of an army through the most desperate venture of the war and on to the most dazzling victory.[37]

Washington led his army across the Delaware to safety but then decided to launch another strike at Princeton, New Jersey. However, by December 29 almost half of his army of twenty-four hun-

A mounted George Washington accepts the surrender of the British after the Battle of Trenton. It was one of Washington's greatest victories.

dred men had left either because there was too little food, they had not been paid, or because their enlistments had expired. During the war many soldiers enlisted for short periods or went home when their families needed them.

On December 29, with one day left in enlistments for most of his army, Washington asked them to stay. But when drums beat to have volunteers reenlist, no one came forward. He then made an emotional plea. "My brave fellows," Washington pleaded, "you have done all I asked you to do, and more than could reasonably be expected. But your country is at stake, your wives, your houses, and all that you hold dear. You have worn yourselves out with fatigues and hardships, but we know not how to spare you." He closed by saying that the nation faced "the crisis which is to decide our destiny."[38]

Moved by his words, freezing, hungry soldiers slowly stepped forward. It was this fierce devotion Washington could inspire that held a rag tag army together at its worst moments during the war. When Private Samuel Downing was 109 years old, he said of Washington, "Oh! but you never got a smile out of him. He was a nice man. *We loved him.* They'd sell their lives for him."[39]

Washington surprised the British again at Princeton on January 3. The two dramatic victories boosted morale throughout the colonies, and that spring eight thousand new recruits enlisted.

The World Turns "Upside Down"

In 1777 superior English forces pushed Washington farther into Pennsylvania; by September, the British had seized Philadelphia. Americans scored a major victory in the Battle of Saratoga, however, when troops led by Major General Horatio Gates stopped a British army trying to invade New York from Canada. Five thousand British soldiers surrendered on October 17.

The winter of 1777–1778 was the low point of the war for Washington and his troops, who endured endless hardships in their primitive winter quarters at Valley Forge, Pennsylvania, located just eighteen miles northwest of Philadelphia. It was not a cold winter, but there were almost no supplies of food, clothing, or medicine; it is believed that three thousand men died at Valley Forge that winter due to typhoid and smallpox epidemics.

Soldiers lived in log huts that they built themselves, and they often had nothing to eat but "fire cake," a mixture of grain and water molded on a stick or in a pan and baked in a campfire. Many soldiers had no coats, hats, or shoes, and their legs and feet froze and turned black; some even had arms or legs amputated. A diary kept by Dr. Albigence Waldo of the First Connecticut Infantry shows the depth of that winter's misery:

George Washington towers over the marquis de Lafayette as they inspect soldiers at Valley Forge. A lack of adequate supplies created unbelievable hardships that winter for the American army.

It snows. I'm sick. Eat nothing. No whiskey. No forage. Lord, Lord, Lord . . . cold and uncomfortable. I am sick, discontented, and out of humor. Poor food. Hard lodging. Cold weather. Fatigue. Nasty clothes. Nasty cookery. Vomit half my time. Smoked out of my senses [by fires to keep warm]. The Devil's in it. I can't endure it. Why are we sent here to starve and freeze? What sweet felicities I have left at home, a charming wife, pretty children, good beds, good food, good cookery. . . . Here all confusion, smoke and cold, hunger and filthiness. A pox on my bad luck.[40]

Although the situation appeared bleak to Washington, the year 1777 was the turning point in the war. The effectiveness of the American army in battling the British led France, Great Britain's traditional enemy, to side with America. Benjamin Franklin negotiated the Treaty of Alliance, which, in early 1778, brought needed French supplies, troops, and military ships to America.

During the next three years, Washington forced the British to retreat in the north to New York City. But the British carried the fighting to Virginia and other southern states and with Native American allies waged a bloody war against settlers in wilderness areas. With the two sides seemingly stalemated, Washington knew he needed a decisive victory to win the war. He got it at Yorktown, Virginia, in 1781.

In a masterpiece of military execution, Washington moved a combined force of seventeen thousand French and colonial troops from New York to Virginia in August to attack Lord Charles Cornwallis. With the aid of French military ships, Washington trapped Cornwallis in the port city and forced him to surrender on October 7, 1781, exactly four years after the British surrender at Saratoga. As British troops filed out of Yorktown, drummers played "The World Turned Upside Down" and soldiers sang,

If ponies rode men and if grass ate cows,
And cats should be chased into holes by the mouse.
If summer were spring and the other way round,
Then all the world would be upside down.[41]

It would take two more years to forge a peace agreement, but the world, indeed, had turned topsy-turvy. The United States had won its freedom.

Creating a New Nation

The victory was bittersweet for Washington. His stepson, John Custis, who had watched the siege of Yorktown from behind

Lord Cornwallis (right) ritually offers his sword to George Washington while surrendering after the Battle of Yorktown. The U.S. victory was the decisive engagement of the American Revolution.

American lines, became ill from a camp virus, probably malaria, and died two weeks later. Although Washington wanted to go home, he led the army for two more years. Before relinquishing command in June 1783, he warned the thirteen states that the military victory was meaningless unless America learned to effectively govern itself:

> This is the moment when the eyes of the whole world are turned upon [you]. This is the moment to establish or ruin [your] national character forever. This is the favorable moment to give such a tone to our federal government as will enable it to answer the ends of its institutions. Or this may be the ill-fated moment for relaxing the powers of the Union [and] annihilating the cement of the Confederation. It is yet to be decided whether the Revolution must ultimately be considered as a blessing or a curse; a blessing or a curse not to the present age alone, for with our fate will the destiny of unborn millions be involved.[42]

Washington joyfully returned to Mount Vernon but continued to worry about the fledgling nation. By 1786, when federal revenues totaled less than one-third of the annual interest owed on the national debt and some Massachusetts farmers had rebelled against paying taxes, Washington realized something had to be done. "I do not conceive," he said, "we can long exist as a nation without a [governmental] power that will pervade the whole union."[43]

The Constitutional Convention

Long an advocate of a stronger central government, Washington was chosen president of the Constitutional Convention on May 14, 1787, in Philadelphia. He made few specific proposals, but his stature and force of personality helped delegates divided on critical issues make necessary compromises. "If to please the people, we offer them what we ourselves disapprove," he told delegates, "how can we defend our work? Let us raise a standard to which the wise and honest can repair. [It] is in the hand of God."[44] According to Richard Norton Smith, director of the Gerald R. Ford Museum, "If Washington had not presided over the [convention], it almost certainly would have come apart at the seams."[45]

Washington's support of the Constitution helped secure its acceptance. His backing was vital for one reason: Many Americans feared the newly created president would be too powerful and rule like a king, and the nation had just fought a war to overthrow such a ruler. But because Washington was expected to become the first president and because he was revered and loved by all, the nation was willing to accept such a powerful figure.

George Washington, standing behind the desk on the platform, was a key figure at the Constitutional Convention. His support for the Constitution helped win its approval by the colonies.

Americans did not fear Washington in part because he had already turned down a chance to become king. After the victory at Yorktown, some of his officers believed the country would be better off with Washington as king or dictator. On May 22, 1782, Colonel Lewis Nicola of Pennsylvania wrote to Washington saying he and other officers would help him seize control of the Continental army so he could win control of the nation. In a letter to Nicola, Washington angrily rejected the offer:

> I read with attention the sentiments you have submitted to my perusal. Be assured, Sir, no occurrence in the course of the War has given me more painful sensations than your information of there being such ideas existing in the army as you have expressed, and I must view [them] with abhorrence and reprehend [you] with severity. If I am not deceived in myself, you could not have found a person to whom your schemes were more disagreeable. . . . Banish these thoughts from your mind, and never communicate, as from yourself, or any one else, a sentiment of like nature.[46]

President Washington

On April 14, 1789, Washington was elected president by the electoral college with sixty-nine votes, and John Adams finished second with thirty-four votes to become vice president; both men were reelected four years later. While awaiting word of voting at Mount Vernon, Washington wrote that his feelings were "not unlike those of a culprit who is going to the place of his execution."[47]

On April 30 in New York, Washington was sworn in as the first president of the United States. New York chancellor Robert R. Livingston read the oath: "Do you solemnly swear that you will faithfully execute the office of president of the United States and will, to the best of your ability, preserve, protect, and defend the Constitution of the United States?" "I solemnly swear," replied Washington, repeating the oath word for word. He then added, on his own, "So help me God,"[48] a postscript adopted by every other president since.

The Constitution provided a structural framework, but Washington and others had to hammer out details of organization, procedure, and protocol that fixed the machinery of government for all time. Even so simple a thing as what to call Washington had to be decided—a congressional committee unsuccessfully recommended "His Highness, the President of the United States of America and Protector of Their Liberties." "President" was good enough for Washington.

One of Washington's most important decisions was to create a cabinet, the department heads who began to meet with him regularly to report on their operations and consult with him on various issues. Presidents today still appoint cabinet members to run various agencies and to advise them on key issues.

In August 1789 Washington conferred with the Senate about a Native American treaty; he became furious because senators could not make a decision after a full day of deliberations. "This defeats every purpose of my coming here,"[49] the president said as he stalked out of the meeting. Washington decided to negotiate the treaty himself and then let the Senate vote on it, another practice continued to the present day.

In April 1792 Washington used the presidential veto for the first time to reject a bill that would have reapportioned congressional seats based on the 1790 census, which showed a population of nearly 4 million people, including 700,000 slaves. Washington vetoed it because he believed it gave too many new seats to northern states. When the House failed to override the veto, a new plan was drawn up.

George Washington (right) takes the oath of office April 30, 1789, to become the first president of the United States.

More important than any specific presidential act was the fact that Washington's stature helped win public support for the presidency and the new government. Historian Margaret L. Coit maintains, "What Washington sensed, instinctively and correctly, was that in his own person he must symbolize the majesty and authority of the central government. What counted was not what he did so much as what he was, the symbol that the people chose to make of him."[50]

The Death of a Founding Father

After eight years as president, Washington left Philadelphia in March 1797 to retire to Mount Vernon and the simple pleasures of farming he so enjoyed.

It was snowing and uncommonly cold on the morning of December 13, 1799, only thirty degrees, but wintry weather could not stop Washington from riding out to check on work being done. Late that afternoon he returned home soaking wet and with snow

Farewell Address

In his famous farewell address, George Washington gave his countrymen some final words of advice. The address was not delivered orally but instead printed in newspapers, appearing first on September 17, 1796, in the American Daily Advertiser *in Philadelphia. His speech is reprinted in* The American Reader.

Washington warned Americans against competition between political parties, saying conflicting claims and arguments parties might raise on issues could hurt and perhaps even destroy national unity.

"You cannot shield yourselves too much against the jealousies & heart burnings which spring from these misrepresentations. They tend to render alien to each other those who ought to be bound together by fraternal affection. To the efficacy and permanency of your union, a government for the whole is indispensable. No alliances between the parts can be an adequate substitute."

The Constitution, he said, was a sacred law that must always be followed.

"The basis of our political systems is the right of the people to make and to alter their constitutions of government. But the Constitution which at any time exists, 'till changed by an explicit and authentic act of the whole people, is sacredly obligatory upon all. The very idea of the power and the right of the people to establish government presupposes the duty of every individual to obey the established Government."

Washington said the United States should "cultivate peace & harmony with all [nations]" but warned it should never become aligned too strongly with one nation because it could then be dragged into that country's conflicts with other nations: "'Tis our true policy to steer clear of permanent Alliances, with any portion of the foreign World. . . . Taking care always to keep ourselves, by suitable establishments, on a respectably defensive posture, we may safely trust to temporary alliances for extraordinary emergencies."

Washington's last piece of advice resulted in an isolationist policy in the United States for more than a century, a period in which America always tried to remain neutral when other countries went to war.

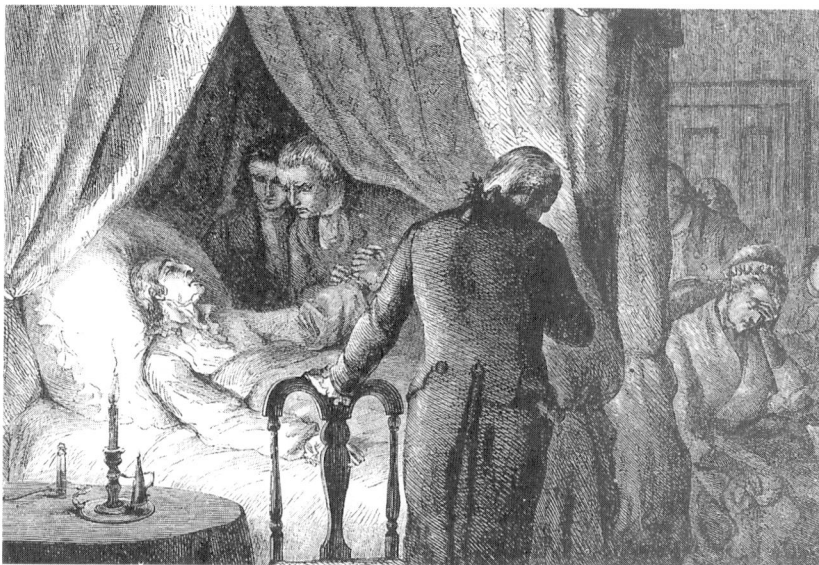

As doctors try vainly to save his life, George Washington lies on his deathbed. The man called the "father of his country" died December 14, 1799.

clinging to his white hair; he ate dinner without changing. That night he woke up at 3 A.M.—he was having trouble breathing, his throat was sore, and he could hardly talk.

Doctors were summoned, but Washington continued to weaken. When more doctors came later in the day, Washington became angry, saying he wanted to "be permitted to die without further interruptions." He told his secretary, Tobias Lear, "I am just going. Have me decently buried and not let my body be put into the vault in less than three days after I am dead." Lear nodded, but Washington rasped, "Do you understand?" "Yes sir!" Lear replied. Washington then spoke his final words: "'Tis well."[51]

Washington died at 10 P.M. on December 14 with Martha at his side. Upon his death, Washington freed his 124 slaves.

CHAPTER 3

Benjamin Franklin: The Most Famous Colonial

Benjamin Franklin, who was sixty-nine when American and British soldiers clashed at Lexington in 1775, was the elder statesman among America's founders. Franklin was also the most famous, renowned in Europe for his scientific experiments, skill as a writer, and forceful defense of the rights of colonists seeking freedom from their English masters.

Born on January 17, 1706, in Boston, Massachusetts, the fifteenth child and tenth son of a soap and candle maker, and the youngest son of a youngest son for five generations, Franklin rose from humble origins to master a wide variety of disciplines and become rich and famous. Biographer Alfred Tamarin sums up his brilliant life:

> Benjamin Franklin was the first American to become a world figure. From an ambitious young man with a bent for self-education and self-advertisement he became a world famous scientist, inventor, legislator, diplomat, and statesman. He was the genius of electricity, and the only figure whose name appears on all four of the major documents of the founding of the United States: the Declaration of Independence, the Constitution, the Treaty of Alliance with France, and the Treaty of Peace with England.[52]

Franklin was the prototype of the American success story: the individual who by hard work and natural talent rose to heights of greatness.

Franklin's Youth

Josiah Franklin came to Boston from England in 1683 with his wife, Anne, and three children. A dyer by trade, he turned to making soap and candles because Boston's Quakers shunned the frivolity of bright colors for clothing. When Anne died, Josiah remarried and had ten children with his second wife, Abiah.

The Franklin home was crowded and happy, but mealtimes could be lengthy. While helping his father salt a winter supply of meat, young Ben once asked: "Father, why don't you say grace right now over the whole pig, and then we won't have to say it over every piece at meals?"[53] The suggestion, ignored by his pious father, showed that Franklin was already developing a mind that would not hesitate to ignore convention if he could find a better way to do things.

As a youngster, Franklin enjoyed swimming, but even then his amazing intellect came into play. He discovered that if he flew a kite while swimming, the wind would propel him through the water. He also invented devices to help him swim faster:

This modest wooden home in Boston was the birthplace of Benjamin Franklin.

> When I was a boy, I made two oval palettes, each about ten inches long and six broad, with a hole for my thumb, in order to retain it fast in the palm of my hand. They much resembled a painter's palettes. In swimming I pushed the edges of these forward, and I struck the water with the flat surfaces as I drew them back. I remember I swam faster by means of these palettes. I also fitted to the soles of my feet a kind of sandals.[54]

Printer's Assistant

As a child, Franklin helped his father make candles and soap; at age twelve, however, he became an apprentice to his half brother James, who was a printer. Ben went to work early each morning, readying supplies of ink and type and setting up the primitive printing press that could print only one page at a time. In love with the written word, Franklin enjoyed hauling down the huge wooden lever to press the paper on the type, which he had coated with ink, and creating a printed page: "From my infancy, I was passionately fond of reading, and all the little money that came into my hands was laid out in the purchasing of books."[55]

Young Franklin read everything he could find, from the Greek philosopher Plato to grammar and arithmetic texts, and he learned to use words as tools to win arguments or make jokes.

Historians John A. Garraty and Robert A. McCaughey explain how Franklin worked hard to become a good writer:

Young Benjamin Franklin works as a printer's apprentice. He would soon be writing articles as well as printing them.

To improve his style, Ben practiced writing by the hour. He would read over a passage he admired in a book or article, making notes (he called them "short hints") on its contents. He would then put the notes aside for a few days and then used them to try to reconstruct the passage. By comparing the result with the original, he learned to correct awkward phrases and imprecise passages in his work. Another somewhat more difficult technique was to turn the passages into verse, and later turn the verse back into prose in the same manner.[56]

In 1721 his brother James founded the *New England Courant*. Ben helped print and deliver the newspaper and secretly began writing articles for it, slipping them under the door of the print shop because he believed James would reject them if he knew who the author was. Ben used the pen name Silence Dogood, a fictional widow who commented comically on local events.

When his brother was jailed for a month in 1722 for criticizing colonial authorities, Franklin published the paper himself. Silence Dogood commented angrily on James's arrest: "Without freedom of thought there can be no such thing as wisdom, and no such thing as public liberty without freedom of speech. . . . Whoever would overthrow the liberty of a nation must begin by subduing the freeness of speech."[57] Freedom was already important to the teenage Franklin.

Philadelphia

The brothers had a falling out after James was freed, and Franklin left to seek his fortune. After a long, difficult journey, a tired, dirty, and shabbily dressed Franklin arrived in Philadelphia in October 1723. But in *Benjamin Franklin: A Biography,* Ronald W. Clark claims Franklin was already on his way to fame and fortune:

Yet when he stepped ashore at Market Street Wharf, Franklin had characteristics which more than outweighed his poverty. He was only an inch or two less than six feet in height, thickset and muscular, with dark brown hair above friendly hazel eyes. He was obviously able to look after himself, a distinct advantage in the rougher eighteenth century, and of use even today. These physical attributes were compounded by a nimbleness of mind, so that in [mind] as well as in action he tended to be off the mark quicker than most men. Above all, and largely concealed by his instinctive hail-fellow-well-met nature, there was a steely determination to succeed and some impatience with those who got in the way.[58]

Franklin served as a printer's assistant in Philadelphia for a year before traveling to London, where he spent two years learning more about printing and read widely to continue his education. English printers called Franklin "the water American" because he drank water instead of the six pints of beer that was a staple of their own daily diet.

Returning to Philadelphia in October 1726, Franklin opened his own business, printing everything from newspapers, books, stationery, and pamphlets to colonial currency. In 1728 Franklin bought the *Pennsylvania Gazette*, a dull weekly newspaper he popularized with his humorous commentary. His greatest success was *Poor Richard's Almanack*, an annual collection of weather predictions, jokes, recipes, and health remedies. The almanac included the witty short sayings that established Franklin's reputation as a moral philosopher and keen commentator on human nature, such as, "He that lies down with dogs, shall rise up with fleas."[59]

> **Poor Richard, 1733.**
>
> A N
> # Almanack
> For the Year of Chrift
> # 1 7 3 3,
> Being the Firft after LEAP YEAR:
>
> | | |
> |---|---|
> | *And makes fince the Creation* | Years |
> | By the Account of the Eastern *Greeks* | 7241 |
> | By the Latin Church, when ⊙ ent. ♈ | 6932 |
> | By the Computation of *W. W.* | 5742 |
> | By the *Roman* Chronology | 5682 |
> | By the *Jewish* Rabbies | 5494 |
>
> *Wherein is contained*
> The Lunations, Eclipfes, Judgment of the Weather, Spring Tides, Planets Motions & mutual Afpects, Sun and Moon's Rifing and Setting, Length of Days, Time of High Water, Fairs, Courts, and obfervable Days.
> Fitted to the Latitude of Forty Degrees, and a Meridian of Five Hours Weft from *London*, but may without fenfible Error, ferve all the adjacent Places, even from *Newfoundland* to *South-Carolina*.
>
> By *RICHARD SAUNDERS*, Philom.
>
> PHILADELPHIA:
> Printed and fold by *B. FRANKLIN*, at the New Printing-Office near the Market.

Benjamin Franklin's provocative sense of humor helped make Poor Richard's Almanack *a publishing sensation.*

Poor Richard's Almanack

The wit and wisdom of Benjamin Franklin is probably best known through the short sayings he sprinkled through volumes of Poor Richard's Almanack, *which was printed annually from 1733 until 1758. It was named after the fictional Richard Saunders, the alleged publisher who was poor. Here is a sampling of Franklin's wit and wisdom from* The American Reader.

"Early to bed and early to rise, makes a man healthy, wealthy, and wise.

God helps them that help themselves.

Don't throw stones at your neighbors, if your own windows are glass.

Teach your child to hold his tongue; he'll learn fast enough to speak.

He that cannot obey, cannot command.

He that waits upon a fortune, is never sure of a dinner.

Three may keep a secret if two of them are dead.

Fish and visitors stink in 3 days.

Diligence is the mother of Good Luck.

The noblest question of the world is, *What good may I do in it?*

Wink at small faults; remember you have great ones.

Little strokes, fell great oaks.

No gains without pains.

One today is worth two tomorrows."

Scientist and Inventor

With financial independence, Franklin was free to do what he wanted: study electricity, tinker with inventions, find new ways to improve life in Philadelphia, and spend more time with his family.

In 1730 he married Deborah Read. It was a common-law marriage, not recognized legally because Deborah had married previously but never divorced her husband, who had deserted her. In 1731 Franklin's son, William, was born. Although the Franklins raised him, historians question whether Deborah was his mother. In any event, William was born illegitimately and went on to father an illegitimate son of his own, William Temple Franklin.

Historian Richard B. Morris writes that the great contradiction about Franklin is "how the popularizer of an American code of hard work, frugality, and moral restraint [could have] no conscientious scruples about enjoying high living, a liberal sexual code for himself, and bawdy humor."[60] Throughout his life, Franklin ignored social conventions.

Despite his love of frivolity, Franklin's inquiring mind was always working. Once, while listening to English evangelist George Whitefield speak outdoors in Philadelphia, Franklin walked as far down the street as he could and still hear the preacher. Franklin then imagined a semicircle with a radius of the distance he had paced off, allowed each listener two square feet of space, and calculated that more than thirty thousand people could have heard Whitefield. "This," he wrote, "reconcil'd me to newspaper accounts of his having preach'd to 25,000 people . . . and to the ancient histories of generals haranguing whole armies, of which I had sometimes doubted."[61]

Franklin's overpowering curiosity about nearly everything he encountered in life, one of his most valuable traits, led him to investigate natural phenomena such as electricity. To test his theory that lightning and electricity were the same physical force, he devised a famous experiment. In June 1752 Franklin and William flew a kite during a thunderstorm. Franklin attached a metal key to the kite string; when he touched it, a small electrical spark was transmitted to his finger. When the results of his research were published in England as a book titled *Experiments and Observations on Electricity Made at Philadelphia by Mr. Benjamin Franklin*, he became famous for his intellect at a time when Europeans viewed Americans as unrefined and uneducated.

Franklin valued knowledge for its practical applications as much as for its own sake. He used what he learned about electricity to invent the lightning rod, which protected homes during storms. Other inventions included bifocals, eliminating the need for people to carry one pair of glasses for reading and a second pair for distance vision, and the Franklin stove, a major advance in the ease and efficiency of heating. For his personal use, Franklin built a foot-operated fan in his study and a book rest that enabled him to read while soaking in his bathtub.

Public Servant

In 1727 Franklin started the Junto, a club whose members wrote and discussed essays on various topics. Known first as the Leather Apron Club since many members were young apprentices, the group gradually evolved into an intercolonial group called the American Philosophical Society, which still exists today. Members of the Junto worked to improve life in Philadelphia. They started the city's first public library; organized the City Watch, a forerunner of today's police departments; and created the Union Fire Company, the world's first city fire department.

A Shocking Experiment

Ben Franklin's experiments with electricity not only made him famous, they nearly killed him. After he learned how to produce electricity, Franklin demonstrated this strange new power for people in a number of ways, including conducting electricity into the bodies of birds to kill them. The object of the experiment was to show his audience how strong and deadly electricity was. In his autobiography, which he began writing in 1771 in the form of letters to his son, William, Franklin describes an experiment that went wrong.

"I have lately made an experiment in electricity that I desire never to repeat. Two nights ago being about to kill a turkey by the shock from two large glass jars containing as much electrical fire [a name then for electricity] as forty common phials, I inadvertently took the whole thro' my own arms and body, by receiving the fire from the united top wires with one hand, while the other held a chain connected with the outsides of both jars.

The company present (whose talking to me, and to one another I suppose occasioned my inattention to what I was about) say that the flash was very great and the crack as loud as a pistol; yet my senses being instantly gone, I neither saw the one nor heard the other; nor did I feel the stroke on my hand, tho' I afterwards found it raised a round swelling where the fire enter'd as big as half a pistol bullet, by which you may judge of the quickness of the electrical fire, which by this instance seems to be greater than that of sound, light and animal sensation."

In June 1752, Benjamin Franklin and his son, William, fly a kite in one of science's most famous experiments.

Benjamin Franklin was the nation's first political cartoonist. Appearing May 9, 1754, in the Pennsylvania Gazette, *this cut-up snake symbolizes why it was important for the colonies to be united.*

In 1736 Franklin became clerk of the Pennsylvania General Assembly and the next year Philadelphia's deputy postmaster. In 1748 he sold his printing business; two years later he was elected to the Pennsylvania Assembly, where he served until 1764. He became postmaster general for the colonies in 1753, and one year later he was the Pennsylvania delegate to the intercolonial congress at Albany, New York, which met to consider how to deal with the threat of the French and Indian War.

In Albany he proposed the Albany Plan of Union, one of the first calls to unify the colonies. When Governor William Shirley of Massachusetts proposed an alternate plan, Franklin criticized it: "Excluding the people of the colonies from all share in the choice of a grand council would probably give extreme dissatisfaction, as well as taxing them by act of Parliament, where they have no representatives."[62] Franklin thus defined the major cause of the American Revolution more than two decades before it started.

Colonial Agent

Pennsylvania, a "proprietary" rather than a "royal," colony, was owned and governed not by King George II (reigned 1727–1760) but by Thomas Penn, son of founder William Penn, to whom King Charles II (reigned 1660–1685) had granted 15 million acres of land.

As early as 1747, when Penn refused to authorize a militia to defend the colony against attacks by French and Native American forces, Franklin wrote, "*Protection* is as truly due from the government to the people, as *Obedience* from the people to the government."[63]

Although Franklin loved and respected the British, he began to believe America would be better off governing itself. In 1757 he went to England to argue for more colonial freedom and stayed six years representing Pennsylvania, and later Georgia, New Jersey, and Massachusetts, on various issues. Franklin returned to Philadelphia in 1762 having swayed some English officials with his arguments on behalf of the colonies. William, who had accompanied his father to England and made powerful friends, was named royal governor of New Jersey, an honor that would eventually place father and son on opposite sides in the Revolution. The war also divided many other families and friends, making them enemies in the fight for independence. Known as Loyalists, these colonists who supported Great Britain during the Revolution were treated harshly after the war, and some of them left the new nation to settle in Great Britain.

In 1764 Franklin returned to London and became a celebrated spokesman for colonial rights. Although Franklin failed to prevent passage of the Stamp Tax in 1765, the following year his eloquent arguments helped persuade Parliament to repeal the act when he convinced British legislators that Americans would never pay the hated tax. "No, never," he said, "unless compelled by force of arms." When asked, "What used to be the pride of the Americans?" Franklin answered, "To indulge in the fashions and manufactures of Great Britain." Asked, "What is now their pride?" Franklin boldly stated, "To wear their old cloths over again, 'til they can make new ones."[64] Franklin's testimony helped win repeal by pointing out that the American embargo of British goods was hurting the English economy.

"We Must All Hang Together"

Franklin remained in England for nearly a decade, defending colonial rights while trying to ease the growing friction between colony and mother country. When he finally realized that war was inevitable, he returned home in May 1775 and became a delegate to the Second Continental Congress. Committed to the fight for freedom, Franklin fought attempts by some to end the war and allow Great Britain to continue ruling America. "They that give up essential liberty to obtain a little temporary safety deserve neither liberty nor safety,"[65] he proclaimed.

When Franklin returned home, he tried to win his son over to the American side. Franklin had already written to him from England saying, "I think independence more honorable than any service [to Great Britain]" and warning William that "you will find yourself in no comfortable situation"[66] once war begins. William ignored his father's advice and was imprisoned during the war.

Franklin resumed his duties as postmaster general of the colonies, became president of the Pennsylvania Constitutional Convention, and was an important member of Congress. He served on a variety of committees, and in 1776 he was named along with John Adams and Thomas Jefferson to write the Declaration of Independence. Signing the document was a bold, dangerous step because Great Britain would consider anyone who did so a traitor. The penalty for treason was death.

The Franklin Stove

Perhaps Ben Franklin's most practical invention, one that changed the way people lived more than any other, was the Pennsylvania fireplace, later known as the Franklin stove. Franklin biographer Ronald W. Clark explains this important technological breakthrough.

"By the 1740s the colonial population was beginning to burn up available forest fuel and heating was growing more expensive. Franklin estimated that five-sixths of the heat was being lost up the chimney. The Pennsylvania Fire Place incorporated passages and vents to draw cold fresh air from outside the building and, after warming the air in passages kept hot by the escaping gases of the fire, finally discharged it into the room. Franklin said the stove's main advantage was that 'your whole room is equally warmed, so that people need not crowd round the [fireplace], but may sit near the window, and have the benefit of the light for reading, writing, needle-work, [and other things]. They may sit with comfort in any part of the room, which is a very considerable advantage in a large family, where there must often be two fires kept, because all cannot conveniently [gather around] one.'"

Franklin made the first stove, the predecessor of today's furnaces, of cast iron in the early 1740s. Although Franklin could have become rich from his invention, he refused to patent the idea because "as we enjoy great advantages from the inventions of others, we should be glad of an opportunity to serve others by any invention of ours, and this we should do freely and generously."

At the formal signing on August 2, John Hancock urged his colleagues to put their signatures on the radical document because "we must all hang together." Franklin wryly quipped, "Yes, we must indeed all hang together, or most assuredly we shall all hang separately."[67]

Diplomat of the Revolution

In September, Franklin went to France along with Arthur Lee and Silas Deane to seek financial and military aid for the war. It was there that Franklin made his greatest contribution to the American Revolution, helping convince the French to side with America against England, its traditional enemy.

Although he was becoming frail at age seventy, Franklin secured aid that perhaps no other American could have won for one simple reason: The French adored him. His scientific reputation, wit, and gracious manners made him a star attraction in political, literary, and social circles. When Queen Marie Antoinette, who a few years later was beheaded in the French Revolution, called him *l'ambassador electrique*, Franklin brazenly told the queen that her eyes "do more mischief in a week than I have done in all my experiments."[68] His cavalier, slightly racy remarks only made him more popular.

A French noblewoman teases Benjamin Franklin for not wearing a powdered white wig. Despite his unstylish mode of dress, Franklin was extremely popular while serving as an ambassador to France.

Franklin, to his own amazement, was treated like a celebrity. It became stylish to display a bust of his head in French homes, and his face and figure were stamped on jewelry, clothing, plates, and medallions that the French rushed to purchase. In most such caricatures, Franklin wore the frontier-style fur hat that so amused the French. "I have, at the request of friends, sat so much and so often for painters and statuaries, that I am perfectly sick of it," Franklin complained. "I know of nothing so tedious as sitting hours in one fix'd posture."[69]

Such adulation, however, helped Franklin win support for America. On February 6, 1778, he negotiated the economic and military alliance with France that would prove to be a turning point in the Revolutionary War. From 1776 to 1783, Franklin also won grants and loans from King Louis XVI to pay for vital military supplies and to enable privateers like John Paul Jones to conduct daring naval raids against Great Britain.

In August 1781 Franklin, John Adams, and John Jay were selected to negotiate a peace treaty with Great Britain. Franklin was the lone peace commissioner for the first three months and played a key role throughout the talks, which culminated in the Treaty of Paris, signed September 3, 1783. "May we never see another war!" Franklin said. "For in my opinion there never was a good war or a bad peace."[70]

Constitutional Convention

Franklin returned home in early 1785 and, despite his age, remained active in public affairs. He served as president of the Pennsylvania executive council for two years, and in 1787, at age eighty-one, he was selected as a delegate to the Constitutional Convention. Hard of hearing and in frail health from a variety of ailments including gout and kidney stones, his wit and wisdom nevertheless helped to calm many angry debates. And Franklin was to provide the inspiration for a compromise that may have saved the convention.

When delegates met May 25, it took them only five days to decide to scrap the Articles of Confederation and draft the Constitution, dramatically different in its creation of a much stronger central government. As a result of a massive shift of authority from the state to the federal level, the national government would now have the power to levy taxes, regulate interstate and foreign commerce, and raise and maintain an army and a navy. States would no longer be able to issue money, make treaties, or tax imports or exports.

The convention almost fell apart when large and small states split over two opposing plans on how to apportion seats in Congress. James Madison, a future president who was one of the key figures in drafting the Constitution, presented the Virginia Plan, which favored large, more populous states by calling for representation in both the House of Representatives and the Senate based on population. Small states, fearing this would allow large states to dominate the government, countered with William Patterson's New Jersey Plan, which proposed a unicameral legislature in which each state had a single vote.

When the states deadlocked on the issue, a Grand Committee consisting of one man from each state was selected to work out a compromise. Historian Thomas Fleming notes that when they met July 4, Franklin played the role of peacemaker in hammering out a grand compromise:

> Benjamin Franklin, who had said almost nothing thus far, found the Grand Committee the ideal place to wield his formidable diplomatic powers. He seized on an idea that had been proposed by [Connecticut delegate] Roger Sherman in an early debate: Each state should have an equal vote in the upper house and proportional representation in the lower house. Shrewdly, Franklin suggested a concession to the large states: All money bills would originate in the lower house. The proposal won the Grand Committee's unanimous support.[71]

Benjamin Franklin's stout figure, bald head, and plain features belie his adventurous, humorous personality and quick intelligence. He was one of the most interesting people in his era.

When the convention ended, not all delegates were satisfied with the proposed Constitution, which still faced a difficult battle for ratification. In a speech on September 17, 1787, Franklin admitted, "There are several parts of this Constitution which I do not at present approve."[72] But he pleaded with delegates to back it. "On the whole," he said, "I cannot help expressing a wish that every member of the Convention, who may still have objections to it, would with me, on this occasion, doubt a little of his own infallibility, and to make manifest our unanimity, put his name on this instrument."[73]

His words were all the more poignant because he was too weak to stand up and deliver them; a friend, James Wilson, read the speech.

A "Printer" Dies

Even that speech, which helped solidify support for the Constitution, was not his last accomplishment. His final public act February 12, 1790, was to sign a petition to Congress on slavery, which he characterized as a "detestable commerce," that urged an end to "the traffic in the persons of our fellow men."[74] At the time, Franklin, who once sold slaves himself as part of his many business ventures, was president of the Pennsylvania Abolition Society, the first society in the world seeking to end slavery.

Franklin died two months later on April 17 at age eighty-four. Although his accomplishments were legendary and his titles voluminous, the will he had signed began: "I, Benjamin Franklin, of Philadelphia, printer, late Minister Plenipotentiary from the United States of America to the Court of France, now President of the State of Pennsylvania."[75]

It was his role as a simple printer, from which he began his long journey to fame, fortune, and an honored spot in American history, that was still most dear to him at the end of his life.

CHAPTER 4

Thomas Jefferson: Author of the Declaration of Independence

In 1962 President John F. Kennedy told a group of Nobel Prize winners at a White House dinner, "I think this is the most extraordinary collection of talent, of human knowledge, that has ever been gathered together at the White House—with the possible exception of when Thomas Jefferson dined alone."[76] The whimsical jest was based on the deep respect Kennedy had for Jefferson, one of his political idols. Historian, lawyer, architect, musician, scientist, surveyor, philosopher, diplomat, farmer, author—Jefferson earned all those titles as well as those of governor of Virginia, secretary of state, vice president, and president.

But Jefferson's greatest achievement was the Declaration of Independence, the historic document that was a formal declaration of freedom from Great Britain as well as an elegant, moving avowal of the political philosophy that was the new nation's moral foundation. Its most powerful claim was that "all men are created equal," a revolutionary idea at a time when the Western world was ruled by royal families who enjoyed far greater wealth and privilege than "common" people.

That phrase, however, was not true even in 1776 America, where a half-million men, women, and children, one-fifth of its population, lived as slaves. Jefferson himself owned slaves and, it is believed, fathered at least one child with a slave named Sally Hemings.

Although his conflicting views on equality and his relationship with Hemings have marred Jefferson's reputation, they represent only one small facet of one of the most intriguing, important figures in American history.

Jefferson's Youth

Jefferson was born on April 13, 1743, to Peter and Jane Jefferson on Shadwell, a thousand-acre plantation in Albemarle County, Virginia. His father married into the Randolph family, one of the richest in Virginia, and as members of the plantation aristocracy, the Jeffersons led a comfortable life.

Biographer Don Nardo describes young Jefferson's restless, questioning mind:

> From the time he could walk and talk, he was keenly interested in all of the natural life around him. He spent hours observing birds, forest animals, insects, flowers, and trees. His father encouraged the boy's curiosity to learn. The elder Jefferson taught his young son to carry notebooks everywhere and keep records of his observations. Even at the age of ten, the boy kept unusually detailed and thorough records.[77]

A Jefferson Portrait

Like George Washington, Thomas Jefferson was taller than most men of his era. His imposing height of six feet, two and a half inches and his red hair made him a distinctive figure. In 1790, when Jefferson became secretary of state under President George Washington, Congressman William Maclay wrote his impressions of Jefferson, providing a wonderful portrait of this founding father. The description is taken from Jefferson: A Revealing Biography *by Page Smith.*

"Jefferson is a slender man; has rather the air of stiffness in his manner; his clothes seem too small for him; he sits in a lounging manner, on one hip commonly, and with one of his shoulders elevated much above the other; his face has a sunny aspect; his whole figure has a loose, shackling air. He has a rambling vacant look, and nothing of that firm collected deportment which I expected would dignify the presence of a secretary or minister. I looked for gravity, but a laxity seemed shed about him. He spoke almost without ceasing, but even his discourse partook of his personal demeanor. It was loose and rambling, yet he scattered information wherever he went, and some even brilliant sentiments sparkled from him. The information which he gave us respecting foreign ministers, etc., was all high-spiced. He had been long enough abroad to catch the tone of European folly."

When Jefferson was five years old, his family hired a tutor to teach him and his older sisters, Jane and Mary, mathematics, reading, and writing. When he was nine he studied Latin and Greek at a nearby private school while continuing his informal education by reading everything he could get his hands on. Jefferson studied Virginia's upper class with the same keen eye he applied to other subjects, discovering that people were not necessarily smart or good simply because they were born to rich families. Jefferson said that while growing up he was surrounded by "an artificial aristocracy founded on wealth and birth, without either virtue or talents."[78] The death of his father was a turning point in his life:

This tiny, primitive schoolhouse at Tuckahoe is where Thomas Jefferson first attended school.

When I recollect that at 14 years of age the whole care and direction of myself was thrown on my self entirely, without a relative or friend qualified to advise or guide me, and recollect the various sorts of bad company with which I associated from time to time, I am astonished I did not turn off with some of them, and become as worthless to society as they were. From the circumstances of my position I was often thrown into the society of horse-racers, card players, fox-hunters, scientific and professional men, and of dignified men; and many a time I asked myself . . . well, which of these kinds of reputations should I prefer? That of a horse jockey? A fox-hunter? An orator? Or the honest advocate of my country's rights.[79]

Although Jefferson had written "without a relative," his mother was still alive. Like Washington, Jefferson was never close to his mother, making it easy for him to leave home in 1760 and attend the College of William and Mary in Williamsburg.

Jefferson Becomes a Revolutionary

In college Jefferson's favorite teacher was William Small, a Scottish professor of mathematics. Jefferson later recalled that having

64

Small as a teacher "was my great good fortune and what probably fixed the destinies of my life."[80] Small introduced Jefferson to the ideas and principles of the Enlightenment, the philosophical movement emerging in Europe that emphasized scientific ways of investigating the world and stressed individual freedom. Jefferson and other revolutionaries incorporated Enlightenment principles in devising a new system of government that gave its citizens more personal freedom.

After two years of college, Jefferson then studied law for another five years, a period far longer than normal because he pursued other subjects to satisfy his insatiable craving for knowledge in many subjects. When Jefferson became interested in government, he learned about it firsthand by attending sessions of the Virginia House of Burgesses. It was there that he first heard Patrick Henry, one of colonial America's most impassioned leaders, call for independence.

Jefferson was moved deeply by Henry's oratory and arguments such as "Men are not handicapped by laws passed a hundred or a thousand years ago. Men live in their own times and rule themselves according to their times."[81] It was while listening to Henry, claims historian Page Smith, that "young Jefferson may be said to have become a revolutionary."[82]

In 1768 Jefferson, by then a successful lawyer, was elected to the House of Burgesses. His mother had died in 1765, leaving him responsible for four siblings: twins Anna Scott and Randolph, 10; Lucy, 13; and Elizabeth, 21, who was believed to be retarded. Despite his many duties, in 1767 Jefferson began building a home near Shadwell named Monticello, which means "little mountain" in Italian. Jefferson designed the unique home and its continual renovation consumed him the rest of his life.

Martha Jefferson, one of Thomas Jefferson's three daughters. Her father affectionately called her "Patsy."

In 1772 he married Martha Wayles Skelton, a widow he once described as "the cherished companion of my life."[83] Her four-year-old son, John, died during the first year of their marriage, and only three of their own six children survived childhood: Martha, called Patsy; Mary, called Maria or Polly; and Lucy Elizabeth.

A Virginia delegate to the First Continental Congress, Jefferson prepared for the historic 1774 meeting by writing *A Summary View of the Rights of British America*. The document listed colonial complaints and urged King George III to give Americans more freedom. "Kings are the servants, not the [owners] of the people," Jefferson wrote. "Open your breast, sire, to liberal and expanded thought. Let not the name of George the third be a blot on the page of history."[84] The document made Jefferson famous, setting him on the course of greatness as author of the Declaration of Independence.

Declaration of Independence

In May 1776 Jefferson, at age thirty-two, was the second youngest member of the Second Continental Congress. After Richard Henry Lee of Virginia introduced a resolution on June 7 declaring the colonies free, Jefferson, John Adams, and Benjamin Franklin were appointed to draft a formal declaration. Jefferson actually wrote the document at the insistence of Adams, who told him: "Reason 1st. You are a Virginian and a Virginian ought to appear at the head of this business. Reason 2nd. I am obnoxious, suspected, and unpopular; you are very much otherwise. Reason 3rd. You can write ten times better than I can."[85]

The opening sentences of the Declaration of Independence are the most powerful:

> When in the Course of human events, it becomes necessary for one people to dissolve the political bands which have connected them with another, and to assume among the powers of the earth, the separate and equal station to which the Laws of Nature and of Nature's God entitle them, a decent respect to the opinions of mankind requires that they should declare the causes which impel them to the separation. We hold these truths to be self-evident, that all men are created equal, that they are endowed by their Creator with certain unalienable Rights, that among these are Life, Liberty and the pursuit of Happiness.[86]

In an "indictment section" Jefferson listed more than two dozen complaints about British actions that he believed justified the Revolution. Although Franklin made minor changes and Congress voted for other revisions—changes that Jefferson, his pride

Thomas Jefferson was the main author of the Declaration of Independence. Here Jefferson, holding a draft of the document, consults with Benjamin Franklin (left) and other delegates.

as an author stung, referred to as "mutilations"—the document was clearly Jefferson's. "I did not consider it any part of my charge to invent new ideas," Jefferson said, "but to place before mankind the common sense of the subject in terms so plain and firm as to command their assent. . . . It was intended to express an American mind."[87]

Legislator and Governor

Back in Virginia, Jefferson began to apply the stirring principles he had embodied in the Declaration of Independence, first as a legislator and then as governor from 1779 to 1781. As a lawmaker he helped write the state's constitution, ensured religious freedom by taking away the Anglican Church's status as Virginia's official church, reformed the criminal code, and abolished the traditional right of primogeniture, which entitled the first-born male to inherit his family's entire estate. The abolition of primogeniture split up many large plantations, enabling more people to own land.

Changes in the Declaration

The ideas, language, and emotions that make the Declaration of Independence a magnificent document are clearly the work of Thomas Jefferson. His first draft, however, is not the document Americans know today. It was edited lightly, first in private by Benjamin Franklin and John Adams, then in open discussion by other delegates to the Second Continental Congress.

Catherine Drinker Bowen, in John Adams and the American Revolution, *says it was agonizing for Jefferson to have his words debated, voted on, and in some cases changed by delegates. Adams said Jefferson was "fighting fearlessly for every word" throughout the whole process, at times banging his hickory cane on the floor in anger when phrases he had labored over were cut or changed.*

The following minor changes made to the first few lines of Jefferson's declaration are taken from Drinker's biography of Adams. Jefferson's original wording is in parentheses and the inserted changes are in boldface type.

"When in the course of human events it becomes necessary for (a) **one** people to (advance from that subordination in which they have hitherto remained & to) **dissolve the political bands which have connected them with another, and to** assume among the powers of the earth the (equal & independent) **separate and equal** station to which the laws of nature & of nature's god entitle them, a decent respect to the opinions of mankind requires that they should declare the causes which impel them to (the change) **the separation.**

We hold these truths to be (sacred & undeniable) **self-evident.** . . .

The last change was Dr. Franklin's. Grudgingly, Jefferson confessed to himself that one word, even hyphenated, was bettter than three. Congress, in point of fact, improved the document by every single alteration. Moreover, they shortened rather than expanded it, a feat seldom if ever achieved by parliamentary critics. In the end, however, it was still Jefferson's composition; no one could doubt it. His pen had written it, his spirit brooded over it, giving light to the whole."

This early draft of the Declaration of Independence shows the evolution of one of America's most important documents.

Jefferson became governor as the British were invading Virginia. Since the state's treasury was almost empty and he had few troops to call upon, Jefferson could not stop the British from looting and burning crops and towns. Jefferson, who fled Monticello in the spring of 1781 when 250 redcoats tried to capture him, describes his leisurely escape:

> [After breakfast] a neighbor rode up full speed to inform me that a troop of horse [soldiers] was then ascending the hill to the house. I instantly sent off my family, and after a short delay for some pressing arrangements, I mounted my horse; and knowing that in the public road I should be liable to fall in with the enemy, I went through the woods, and joined my family at the house of a friend, where we dined.[88]

Personal Tragedy

When Jefferson's second term ended on June 1, 1781, he went home to rebuild Monticello and the other plantations he owned, which had all been damaged by war. He also wrote *Notes on the State of Virginia,* a work that made him famous in Europe. Originally intending to simply answer a list of questions from a French diplomat, the work evolved into a wide ranging volume about geography, plants, animals, history, government, political philosophy, and law.

When Martha became ill after the birth of their last child, Jefferson helped nurse his wife, but she never recovered. "For the four months that she lingered," his daughter Patsy wrote, "he was never out of calling. When not at her bed side, he was waiting in a small room which

A silhouette portrait of Martha Jefferson. When she died, Thomas Jefferson vowed to never marry again.

opened immediately at the head of her bed."[89] Martha died on September 6, 1782, and Jefferson vowed never to marry again.

The grief-stricken Jefferson was soon appointed to Congress. Although in office only a few months, Jefferson had two major accomplishments: He proposed the basic outline for the Northwest

Ordinance of 1787, which allowed creation of five new states, including Illinois and Wisconsin; and he also created a new monetary system. Based on the decimal system, Jefferson's units of dollars, dimes, and pennies were much easier for people to use than the English pounds, farthings, and pence.

In May 1784 Congress named Jefferson a special envoy to negotiate trade and commercial treaties with European nations. A year later Jefferson succeeded Benjamin Franklin as U.S. minister to France, where he lived until 1789.

France and Sally Hemings

Jefferson was revered as a hero of the American Revolution at a time when France was going through its own tumultuous fight for freedom. His celebrity helped him forge new agreements with France and other countries.

It was also in France that Jefferson became involved with Hemings in a relationship that even today clouds his reputation. Known as "Dashing Sally" for her vibrant personality, she was a light-skinned beauty with long straight hair. Jefferson's wife had inherited Hemings and other slaves after the death of her father, John Wayles. Hemings was actually Martha's half sister because Wayles was also her father.

After his daughter Lucy died of whooping cough, Jefferson sent for his youngest child, Mary. Hemings, who was only fourteen at the time, accompanied Mary to France in July 1787; Hemings's brother, Peter, was Jefferson's valet. Hemings's third son, Madison, who was born at Monticello in 1805, claimed years later that in France "my mother became Mr. Jefferson's concubine."[90]

Although their relationship first became public while Jefferson was president, historians have long debated whether he and Hemings had children together. But in the November 1998 issue of *Nature*, Eugene A. Foster, a retired pathologist from Charlottesville, Virginia, and other researchers published the results of their study of the genetic makeup of direct male-line descendants of Sally's final son, named Eston Hemings, and Thomas Woodson, a paternal uncle of Jefferson. Foster concludes that the results "provide evidence that [Jefferson] was the biological father of Eston Hemings Jefferson."[91] Jefferson and Hemings may have had other children, but there is no physical evidence proving it.

As shown by this illicit relationship, Jefferson was torn all his life over the question of slavery. Jefferson once said blacks were inferior to whites mentally and physically and, because he was in debt most of his life, he had to depend on slave labor to run his

Nature Magazine Story

The November 1998 issue of Nature *magazine moved the issue of whether Thomas Jefferson and Sally Hemings had children together out of the realm of historical debate and into the laboratory for scientific investigation. Retired pathologist Eugene A. Foster and other researchers claim that the result is proof that Jefferson was "the biological father of Eston Hemings Jefferson."*

Foster and genetic scientists analyzed the Y chromosomes of direct male-line descendants of Eston Hemings and Thomas Woodson, a paternal uncle of Jefferson's; Jefferson himself had no direct male descendants, with the possible exception of children by Hemings. "The simplest and most probable explanations for our molecular findings," the researchers wrote, "are that Thomas Jefferson was the father of Eston Hemings Jefferson." They said the Jeffersons had a rare Y chromosome makeup that was found in Eston's descendants. However, tests of Thomas Woodson and Hemings's first son, who Jefferson was also accused of fathering, failed to prove he was Jefferson's son.

In a second article in Nature, *geneticist Eric S. Lander and Jefferson biographer Joseph J. Ellis tried to provide a historical perspective for the research.*

"[The] findings renew questions about Jefferson's tortured position on slavery. If Jefferson's relationship with Hemings began in the late 1780s, it would mean that he began to back away from a leadership position in the antislavery movement around the time that his affair with Sally Hemings started. Jefferson's stated reservations about ending slavery included a fear that emancipation would lead to racial mixing and amalgamation. His own interracial affair now personalizes this issue, while adding a dimension of hypocrisy.

Over the past 30 years, research into Jefferson has cast a shadow over his credibility as America's prophet of freedom and equality. Recent work has also emphasized his massive personal contradictions and his dexterity at playing hide-and-seek within himself. The new evidence only deepens the paradoxes.

Jefferson is, with Abraham Lincoln and George Washington, one of America's secular saints. His face looks out from the nickel, the two-dollar bill, the memorial [in Washington, D.C.], and Mount Rushmore. His unique capacity to project inspirational words and ideas onto American public life has made him all things to all people. As an icon, Jefferson's legacy has been reinterpreted by every generation. Now, Jefferson reappears to remind us of a truth that should be self-evident. Our heroes—and especially presidents—are not gods or saints, but flesh-and-blood humans, with all of the frailties and imperfections that this entails."

plantations. But his first legislative act at age twenty-four was to introduce a Virginia bill allowing slaveholders to free their slaves at any time; up until then they could only do it for "meritorious service."

Five years later Jefferson blasted slavery as "an infamous practice" and said abolition of slavery was "the great object of desire" by Americans. In his 1820 autobiography, he writes "Nothing is more certainly written in the book of fate, than that these people are to be free,"[92] and he had structured the Northwest Ordinance to prohibit slavery in new states.

In his draft of the Declaration of Independence, Jefferson accused the English king of being responsible for the slave trade, saying he had "waged a cruel war against human nature itself" by "captivating [blacks] and carrying them into slavery in another hemisphere, or to incur miserable death in their transportation hither."[93] Other delegates rejected the argument, but historian Page Smith believes it symbolized Jefferson's inner conflict:

> Reading the bitter and intemperate accusations on the matter of slavery, it is difficult not to feel that they reflected Jefferson's profound revulsion for the slave trade—which had been the basis of his father-in-law's fortune and of which he had been an indirect beneficiary through his wife's estate—and his own guilt at his involvement in a system he abhorred but which he could not escape. Perhaps he was trying, by using the king of England as a scapegoat, to exorcise his own personal demons.[94]

Political Warfare

Returning home from France on December 23, 1789, Jefferson was able to enjoy only a few months at his beloved Monticello before Washington named him the nation's first secretary of state. Jefferson's tenure was highlighted by his political battles with Treasury Secretary Alexander Hamilton. Historian Margaret L. Coit explains their differences:

> From the moment [Jefferson] assumed office in March 1790, to face a towering stack of important documents and a three-week nervous headache, he and Hamilton, by his own account, were "pitted against each other every day in the cabinet like two fighting-cocks." Hamilton favored the bankers and merchants, Jefferson the farmers and plantation owners. Hamilton, almost alone in his time, was aware of the implications of the Industrial Rev-

olution and looked to an industrial America. Jefferson shunned the idea. The Virginian favored the broadest possible extension of democracy. Hamilton looked to a strong government that would put down mob rule and divert man's natural selfishness to the public good.[95]

Their biggest battle was over Hamilton's proposal for a national bank, which he believed necessary for the country's economic strength. Jefferson believed the Constitution did not give the government the power to create the bank, but Congress approved it and Washington signed the measure into law.

The philosophical division between Jefferson and Hamilton, which extended to other issues such as whether the United States should support the French Revolution, led to the creation of the nation's first political parties. The group headed by Jefferson in 1792 became known as the Republican Party; Hamilton's party was the Federalist.

Jefferson resigned at the end of 1793, ending an unhappy period in which he felt "cut off from my family & friends, my affairs abandoned to chaos and derangement; in short, giving everything I love, in exchange for everything I hate."[96]

Vice President

Jefferson, however, did not find peace at Monticello. He worried about the course the nation was taking, juggled his mounting debts (he had to mortgage his slaves for needed funds), and fell into a depression. Years later he warned his daughter Mary not to give into the same mental condition:

> From 1793 to 1797 I remained closely at home, saw none but those who came there, and at length became very sensible of the ill effect it had upon my own mind, and of its direct and irresistible tendency to render me unfit for society. I felt enough of the effect of withdrawing from the world then, to see that it led to an antisocial and misanthropic state of mind, which severely punishes him who gives into it.[97]

Jefferson was saved from despondency by his election in 1796 as vice president. One of four candidates for president, Jefferson became vice president when he finished second to John Adams. Jefferson, a Republican, and Adams, a Federalist, had once been friends but were now political enemies. Adams never consulted Jefferson on issues, and Jefferson wrote to his daughter Martha that "it gives me great regret to be passing my time so uselessly."[98]

Jefferson poured his heart and soul into building Monticello, which means "Little Mountain" in Italian. His lavish spending on his showcase home was one of the main reasons he was deep in debt when he died.

As vice president, Jefferson stood by helplessly as the Federalists, bending to anti-French feeling, nearly went to war with France. In 1789 the Federalists cracked down on those who disagreed with them, mainly Republicans, by passing the Alien and Sedition Acts. The Alien Act restricted the liberty of supposedly pro-Republican foreigners, and the Sedition Act allowed prosecution of anyone who printed false statements critical of government officials. Twenty-five people were prosecuted under the Sedition Act, and all of them were Republican editors and printers.

The Election of 1800

In 1800 something unprecedented occurred: Governmental power changed hands by ballots instead of bullets as Jefferson defeated Adams for president. This bloodless transfer of authority was an important step in the country's political maturation. "The Revolution of 1800," Jefferson wrote, "was as real a revolution in the principles of our government as that of 1776 was in its form; not effected by the sword, as that, but by the rational and peaceful instrument of reform, the suffrage of the people."[99]

The election was especially dramatic because Jefferson and Aaron Burr, a New Yorker whom Republicans favored for vice president, tied with seventy-three electoral votes; Adams had sixty-five. It took a week, and another thirty-six ballots, before the House of Representatives broke the tie and chose Jefferson. The Twelfth Amendment to the Constitution, requiring electors to vote separately for president and vice president, was passed in 1804 to prevent future political stalemates.

Jefferson's inaugural address on March 4, 1801, is considered one of the greatest ever given—Kennedy lamented that his own memorable 1960 inaugural was not as good—because the new president tried to heal the political wounds that had begun to divide the country. "Let us, then, fellow citizens, unite with one heart and one mind," Jefferson said. "Let us restore to social intercourse that harmony and affection without which liberty and even life itself are but dreary things." He said that even though there were two political parties, its members were all Americans who shared a common heritage: "We are all Republicans, we are all Federalists."[100]

Jefferson as President

Jefferson worked to make the government frugal by reducing the size of the army and navy, cutting spending, and trimming the national debt. He let the Alien and Sedition Acts expire in 1803, and he abolished all taxes except for those on imported goods. Although he opposed Hamilton's financial policies, he left them in tact along with other Federalist programs.

The greatest achievement of his presidency was the Louisiana Purchase, which brought into the union all of the land from the Gulf of Mexico north to the Canadian border and from the Mississippi River west to the Rocky Mountains. The United States bought the land from France in 1802 for $15 million, one of the biggest bargains in history. From the new land came the states of Arkansas, Iowa, Louisiana, Missouri, and South Dakota as well as parts of Colorado, Minnesota, Montana, North Dakota, Oklahoma, and Wyoming.

Jefferson had always been intrigued by the vast expanses beyond the colonies, and in 1801 he envisioned a time when "our rapid multiplication will expand itself . . . and cover the whole northern, if not the southern, continent with a people speaking the same language, governed in similar forms and by similar laws."[101] The Louisiana Purchase was an important step in fulfilling that vision.

His foreign policy was less successful, but he kept America neutral during his second term after England and France went to war again in 1803. The Embargo Act of 1807 tried to force both countries to respect U.S. neutrality by restricting trade, but instead the embargo hurt the American economy by restricting foreign trade.

Return to Monticello

Before Jefferson left office in March 1809 at age sixty-six, he wrote a friend that "never did a prisoner, released from his chains, feel such relief as I shall on shaking off the shackles of power."[102] During eight years as president, Jefferson had dealt not only with difficult governmental issues but also with political and personal attacks, including a newspaper story in 1802 that revealed his relationship with Hemings and damaged his reputation.

Thomas Jefferson had strong, handsome features topped by a shock of thick red hair. Tall for his era at six feet, two and a half inches, Jefferson's imposing physical presence corresponded nicely to the forceful power of his intellect and will.

The article, which appeared on September 1 in the *Richmond Recorder,* a Federalist paper, was the first public accusation that Jefferson fathered children with Hemings. It was written by James T. Callender, a journalist of dubious reputation, but Jefferson never publicly responded to the brief, crudely written story:

> It is well known that the man, whom it *delighteth the people to honor,* keeps, and for many years past has kept, as his concubine, one of his own slaves. Her name is SALLY. The name of her eldest son is TOM. His features are said to bear a striking although sable resemblance to those of the president himself. The boy is ten or twelve years of age. His mother went to France in the same vessel with Mr. Jefferson and his two daughters. The delicacy of this arrangement must strike every person of common sensibility.[103]

In his final seventeen years, Jefferson mainly worked to rebuild his plantations and to make improvements to Monticello. His debts continued to mount, in 1815 he had to sell his book collection of more than six thousand volumes to the Library of Congress, which he had authorized in 1800. He received twenty-five thousand dollars, but fifteen thousand of it went to satisfy some of his most pressing debts. His greatest accomplishment in retirement came in 1819, when he helped establish the University of Virginia.

Jefferson died on July 4, 1826. He had been invited to Washington to celebrate the golden anniversary of his greatest triumph, but he was too weak to travel. The following is part of a message he wrote for the special occasion:

> May it [the Declaration of Independence] be to the world what I believe it will be . . . the signal of arousing men to . . . assume the blessing of self government. . . . The general spread of the light of science has already laid open to every view the palpable truth that the mass of mankind has not been born with saddles on their backs, nor a favored few booted and spurred, ready to ride them. For ourselves, let the annual return of this day, forever refresh our recollection of these rights and an undiminished devotion to them.[104]

When Jefferson died, he could not free all his slaves because of debts of more than one hundred thousand dollars. However, Jefferson honored a promise to free Hemings and all her children.

CHAPTER 5

Alexander Hamilton: America's Financial Genius

John Adams once mockingly referred to Alexander Hamilton as "the bastard brat of a Scots pedlar."[105] The small, red-haired, freckled, pugnacious Hamilton was also a notorious womanizer who once confessed that his motto was "All for love."[106] Yet historian Geoffrey C. Ward believes Hamilton was not only "our first and greatest Secretary of the Treasury" but "second perhaps only to [George] Washington, the man most responsible for creating a nation out of 13 mutually antagonistic states."[107]

Hamilton was a revolutionary philosopher, a soldier, a reluctant defender of the Constitution he helped create but did not admire, and a financial genius whose innovative ideas continue to contribute to the nation's economic strength even today. One of the most colorful and talented of America's founders, Hamilton was also one of the most complex, "a bundle of contradictions" according to historians John A. Garraty and Robert A. McCaughey: "Witty, charming, possessed of a mind like a sharp knife, he was sometimes the soul of practicality, sometimes an incurable romantic. No more hardheaded realist ever lived, yet he was quick to resent any slight of his honor, even—tragically—ready to fight a duel despite his abhorrence of the custom of dueling."[108]

Youth

Born on the West Indian island of Nevis on January 11, 1757, Hamilton was the illegitimate son of James Hamilton, a trader whose father was the Scottish laird of Cambuskieth, and Rachel Fawcett Levine, who was still married to Dutch trader John Levine. In 1750 Rachel had deserted Levine and their four-year-old son, Peter, after five years of an unhappy marriage. She and Hamilton had two sons, James in 1753 and Alexander, named after Hamilton's father. Levine did not divorce Rachel until 1759.

After James Hamilton abandoned his family in 1766, Rachel operated a general store in St. Croix. When Rachel died two years later, she left her sons eight slaves and stocks of salt pork, butter, flour, and other goods, only to have her former husband, John Levine, claim the entire estate for their legitimately born son, Peter Levine. Hamilton, at age eleven, was left penniless and alone in the world.

Although his childhood could be likened to that of the unfortunate hero of a Charles Dickens novel, biographer John F. Roche believes Hamilton's difficult early life prepared him for greatness:

> The weight of illegitimacy, abandonment, family tragedy, and poverty that now bore down upon the adolescent Alexander Hamilton was enough to have crushed many a grown man. But Hamilton was not overcome. Rather, these misfortunes served to awaken in him a fierce, driving determination to rise above his background, to prove his personal worth.[109]

Illegitimacy never made Hamilton feel inferior; he often boasted "my blood is as good as that of those who [pride] themselves upon their ancestry."[110]

After their mother's death, Hamilton, who had been taught to read by his mother, attended a small school, and learned to clerk in her store, was apprenticed to the trading house of David Beckman and Nicholas Cruger; his brother was apprenticed to a carpenter. Although Hamilton was

Although born out of wedlock and raised in poverty, Alexander Hamilton never doubted his abilities.

successful, displaying an amazing ability in business and accounting for one so young, he wrote to a cousin that he wanted to accomplish far greater things:

> Ned [Stevens], my ambition is [so] prevalent that I condemn the groveling conditions of a clerk or the like, to which my fortune, etc., condemns me and would willingly risk my life, though not my character, to exalt my station.

I am confident, Ned, that my youth excludes me from any hopes of immediate preferment; but I mean to prepare the way for futurity.[111]

Two key breaks paved the way for success. When Cruger went to New York for five months in 1771, Hamilton impressed him by ably handling his business. Hamilton's second opportunity came in October 1772, when a letter he wrote vividly describing the devastation of St. Croix and neighboring islands by a powerful hurricane was published in the *Danish-American Gazette*:

Good God! What horror and destruction—it's impossible for me to describe—or you to form any idea of it. It seemed as if a total dissolution of nature was taking place. The roaring of the sea and wind—fiery meteors flying about it in the air—the prodigious glare of almost perpetual lightning—the crash of the falling houses—and the ear-piercing shrieks of the distressed, were sufficient to strike astonishment into Angels.[112]

The melodramatic description brought the enterprising young man to the attention of Dr. Hugh Knox, a Presbyterian minister. Realizing that Hamilton had unusual talents, Knox and Cruger decided to send him to college.

Budding Revolutionary

Arriving in America in 1772 at age fifteen, Hamilton studied for two years in Elizabethtown, New Jersey, to prepare for the College of New Jersey (now Princeton). But Hamilton switched to King's College (now Columbia University) in New York because the first school would not allow him to advance from class to class as he proved his proficiency, a seemingly unnecessary delay to this young man in a hurry to be rich and famous.

Devouring books on political philosophy, Hamilton quickly became a supporter of the American Revolution. When a Loyalist criticized the First Continental Congress, Hamilton wrote two powerful pamphlets defending Congress and presenting his own views on independence: *A Full Vindication of the Measures of Congress from the Calumnies of Their Enemies* and *The Farmer Refuted*. Hamilton claimed the colonies could be self-sufficient and argued that Americans had rights the British must honor: "The sacred rights of mankind are not to be rummaged for among old parchments or musty records. They are written, as with a sunbeam, in the whole volume of human nature, by the hand of the divinity itself, and can never be erased or obscured by mortal power."[113]

Aide to Washington

In March 1776 Hamilton was commissioned a captain of artillery. He served with such distinction that a year later General George Washington made him his aide-de-camp with the rank of lieutenant colonel. Washington soon came to rely heavily on the advice of Hamilton, nicknamed "the Little Lion" by other members of the general's staff.

Hamilton yearned for the glory that only battle could confer. In late 1781 he left Washington's staff to command a New York regiment. Just weeks later Hamilton played a key role in the decisive victory at Yorktown by leading a dramatic charge to capture a British fortification. Biographer John F. Roche describes Hamilton's heroics:

Hamilton and Washington Part

Although Alexander Hamilton considered George Washington something of a father figure while serving under him during the Revolutionary War, their parting in 1781 was less than amicable. Hamilton resigned on February 16 partly because he felt Washington had held him back from taking other jobs during the war, particularly with the Continental Congress. Washington had not done that, but their relations became increasingly strained during the war.

Hamilton biographer Nathan Schachner said the final straw came after they exchanged harsh words. On February 16 Hamilton was hurrying downstairs in the army's headquarters to deliver some orders when he met Washington coming up the stairs. When Washington said he wanted to speak to him, Hamilton responded, "I will wait upon you immediately, sir." But when he was delayed in reporting to Washington, the general exploded in anger: "Colonel Hamilton, you have kept me waiting at the head of the stairs these ten minutes. I must tell you, sir, you treat me with disrespect." Hamilton fired back, "I am not conscious of it, sir. But since you have thought it necessary to tell me so, we part." Washington, still angry, answered, "Very well, sir, if it be your choice."

After Washington calmed down, he tried to reconcile with his valuable aide, but Hamilton refused. Hamilton took command of an artillery battalion and went on to glory at Yorktown. After the war the two became close once again and remained so for the rest of their lives.

When darkness fell (October 14), Hamilton led a silent attack on one redoubt; so as not to attract other British troops to the spot, the Americans did not load their arms but relied on the cold steel of their bayonets. Hamilton himself was the first over the parapet, with the others on his heels. In minutes the whole redoubt was overrun. Its commander and seventeen others were captured, while the great bulk of its defenders fled in dismay. The same night, a French force seized the second redoubt. Two days later, [Lord] Cornwallis launched a desperate counterattack but failed to retake either redoubt. Then he surrendered.[114]

Lawyer, Husband, Politician

After the war Hamilton decided to practice law in Albany, New York. In typical Hamilton haste to accomplish an objective, he studied only six months before being admitted to the bar. Hamilton needed a profession because, in 1780, he had married Betsey Schuyler, whose father, Philip, was one of New York's wealthiest and most influential men. Betsey, Hamilton wrote, "is most unmercifully handsome. She has good nature, affability and vivacity. From a professed condemner of Cupid [she] has in a trice metamorphosed me."[115] Marriage into a prominent family gave Hamilton the social standing he craved.

British troops led by Lord Cornwallis (center) surrender at Yorktown, Virginia, to end the Revolutionary War. Alexander Hamilton was a hero in helping win the battle that gave America its freedom.

In June 1782 Hamilton was named "Receiver of Continental Taxes" for New York. He found the job frustrating because the Articles of Confederation gave Congress the right to assess taxes but no power to collect them. Hamilton raised just $6,250, less than 2 percent of the amount Congress requested.

Hamilton quit in August after being elected to Congress, where he preached the need for a stronger central government. As early as 1780 Hamilton had claimed, "The fundamental defect is a want of power in Congress. The Confederation itself is defective and requires to be altered" and argued that "without certain revenues, a government can have no power."[116]

When his term ended in August 1783, Hamilton went back to his law practice and became successful by representing Loyalists. The treaty ending the Revolutionary War included clauses protecting

In 1780, Alexander Hamilton married Betsey Schuyler. His wife's influential family gave Hamilton the social status he had always sought.

them, but the New York legislature had passed a law allowing confiscation of Loyalist property. Hamilton believed in defending Loyalist rights after the war, but noted pragmatically that the cases provided "so plentiful a harvest to us lawyers that we have scarcely a moment to spare from the substantial business of reaping."[117]

Hamilton began corresponding with influential people about the need for a stronger central government to ensure the nation's survival. One of these people was Washington, who agreed wholeheartedly. "No man in the United States," he wrote Hamilton, "is, or can be more deeply impressed with the necessity of a reform in our present Confederation than myself."[118]

On September 4, 1786, Hamilton represented New York at the Annapolis (Maryland) Convention, a meeting on interstate commerce and other issues called by the state of Virginia. When only five of thirteen states sent delegates, Hamilton drafted a resolution for another meeting the following year to "devise such provisions as shall seem to them necessary to render the [Articles of Confederation] adequate to the [demands] of the union."[119] The result would be the U.S. Constitution.

Hamilton and the Constitution

Although the Constitutional Convention in Philadelphia, which began May 25, 1787, was something Hamilton had dreamed of for years, he played only a small role. This was partly due to the fact that the other two New York delegates, Robert Yates and John Lansing, both opposed a strong central government, which meant Hamilton could not cast New York's vote for ideas he backed. Hamilton also lost interest when he realized that the new government that was beginning to emerge in the debates was not as strong as he desired. Biographer Nathan Schachner believes Hamilton "was essentially incapable of compromise. With him, it was *all* or *nothing.*"[120]

In Hamilton's five-hour-long major speech on June 18, he shocked delegates by saying the government should be patterned after the British monarchy, which he considered the best in the world. Hamilton wanted a legislature with two houses, an assembly elected by free males twenty-one years of age or older, whose members would serve three-year terms, and a senate, modeled after Britain's House of Lords, whose members would be selected from the rich and well born and would serve for life; an independent elected chief executive who would serve for life and have the power to veto any legislation; and an independent judiciary.

Historian Richard B. Morris claims the "unfortunate speech" was one of "the greatest indiscretions of his career" because it forever branded Hamilton a monarchist. Thomas Jefferson, his great political enemy, once accused Hamilton of being "not only a monarchist, but for a monarchy bottomed on corruption."[121]

Although Hamilton would later call the Constitution a "frail and worthless fabric" on which to build a nation, he realized it would create a stronger, better government. Casting aside his doubts, Hamilton then did more than anyone else to secure its ratification by the states as the main author of the *Federalist,* a series of eighty-five articles that ran in newspapers from October 27, 1787, through August 15, 1788. Signed simply "Publius," the articles were written by Hamilton, John Jay, and James Madison.

Hamilton authored more than fifty of the essays, including the first one. It appeared in New York City's *Independent Journal* and argued that changes under the Constitution would help the economy and provide safeguards against democracy's "errors and delusions" while insuring that the "ultimate authority [to govern] resides in the people alone."[122] In the final *Federalist* paper, Hamilton wrote: "A *Nation* without a *National Government* is, in my

The Federalist

Although the authorship of some of the eighty-five essays that make up the Federalist *is in doubt, Alexander Hamilton is believed to have written more than fifty of them. The* Federalist *argued convincingly in favor of the new Constitution and was one of the key factors in helping convince states to ratify it.*

The following excerpt is from the introductory essay in the Federalist, *which Hamilton wrote.*

"After an unequivocal experience of the inefficiency of the subsisting federal government, you are called upon to deliberate on a new Constitution for the United States of America. The subject speaks its own importance; comprehending in its consequences nothing less than the existence of the UNION, the safety and welfare of the parts of which it is composed, the fate of an empire in many respects the most interesting in the world.

My countrymen, I own to you that after having given it an attentive consideration, I am clearly of opinion that it is your interest to adopt [the Constitution]. I am convinced that this is the safest course for your liberty, your dignity, and your happiness. I affect not reserves which I do not feel. I will not amuse you with an appearance of deliberation when I have decided. I frankly acknowledge to you my convictions, and I will freely lay before you the reasons on which they are founded. The consciousness of good intentions disdains ambiguity. . . .

I propose, in a series of papers, to discuss the following interesting particulars:—*The utility of the UNION to your political prosperity—The insufficiency of the present Confederation to preserve that Union—The necessity of a government at least equally energetic with the one proposed, to the attainment of this object—The conformity of the proposed Constitution to the true principles of republican government—Its analogy to your own State constitution*—and lastly, *The additional security which its adoption will afford to the preservation of that species of government, to liberty, and to property."*

view, an awful spectacle. The establishment of a Constitution, in time of profound peace, by the voluntary consent of the whole people, is a *prodigy*, to the completion of which I look forward with trembling anxiety." [123]

In arguing forcefully for a document he did not fully accept himself, Hamilton became a major force in winning its ratification by the thirteen states. He also helped convince Washington to accept the presidency, another key factor in preserving the nation in its early years.

Secretary of the Treasury

When Washington named Hamilton treasury secretary on September 3, 1789, the nation's finances were in disorder, public credit was at low ebb, and state economies were still struggling to adjust to changes resulting from independence. The new nation owed more than $11 million to foreign countries and more than $40 million to its own citizens, much of it in securities it had issued to soldiers, farmers, and merchants. But Hamilton, a fiscal genius for his time, now started putting into practice economic ideas he had been formulating for years.

In his *Report on the Public Credit* to Congress on January 14, 1790, Hamilton argued that the federal government should pay all national and state debts resulting from the Revolution. Hamilton's proposal was controversial, partly because speculators had bought up many of the old debts at a fraction of their value in hopes of one day recovering the full amount. Jefferson and others argued this was unfair because speculators were going to profit at the expense of the people to whom the debts were originally owed.

The measure passed when Hamilton won Jefferson over by agreeing to support moving the nation's capital in 1800 from New York to Washington, D.C., a more southern location Jefferson personally desired. The compromise became known as the "dinner table bargain" because the deal was made when Jefferson, Hamilton, and several others met socially to discuss the issue.

Jefferson and Hamilton became political enemies after that, however, partly because Jefferson believed he had been tricked by Hamilton into supporting federal assumption of state debts. Yet the underlying cause of their animosity was their differing political philosophies: Hamilton believed a strong central government should wield great power while Jefferson thought federal officials should have minimal control over states.

Their feud came to a boiling point over Hamilton's next innovation. In December 1790 he proposed creation of a central Bank of the United States to make it easier for businesses to secure loans and to stabilize the economy. Eighty percent of the bank's initial $10 million in stocks would be sold to private individuals, the remainder to the government. Jefferson and some lawmakers were enraged, claiming investors could become rich from a government bank and questioning its legality, but Congress approved it in February 1791.

When Washington hesitated to sign the bill because he was not sure if the measure was constitutional, Hamilton and Jefferson both sent him written arguments. Jefferson claimed it was illegal because the Constitution did not specifically authorize a national bank. He feared that allowing the bank's creation would enable Congress to "take possession of a boundless field of power no longer susceptible of any definition."[124]

In a fifteen-thousand-word essay, Hamilton argued convincingly that the Constitution's doctrine of "implied powers" made creation of the bank legal, arguing there was a clear connection between the purpose of the bill and the powers stated in the Constitution:

Alexander Hamilton's economic ideas made the United States financially stable. His political philosophy shaped the way it is governed even today.

> Every power vested in a government is in its nature *sovereign*, and includes by *force* of the *term*, a right to employ all the *means* requisite and fairly applicable to the attainment of the *ends* of such power, and which are not precluded by restrictions and exceptions specified in the Constitution, or not immoral, or not contrary to the *essential ends* of political society.[125]

Washington agreed with Hamilton, and the bank was successful from the start in helping to stabilize the U.S. economy. In the first major battle over how to interpret the Constitution, Hamilton, who desired more centralized power, was the victor.

Hamilton's third major report, *On the Establishment of a Mint*, followed in January 1791 while the bank charter was still being debated. It called for a national currency to replace individual currencies being used by the states. Unlike his first two proposals, it was readily accepted, and the first U.S. mint was opened in Philadelphia.

Hamilton and Jefferson

The opposing political ideals Hamilton and Jefferson held split the Federalists and led Jefferson in 1792 to head the newly formed Republican Party. Their political philosophies were based, to a great extent, on their personal views of human nature.

Hamilton was more of an elitist, believing that "communities divide themselves into the few and the many. The first are the rich and well born; the others the mass of the people," who he felt were "turbulent and changing"[126] while the upper class was more interested in seeking order. Nearly contemptuous of the masses, Hamilton once said, "The people, Sir, the people is a great beast!"[127]

But Jefferson, who believed in the ability of the common man to govern, favored the broadest possible extension of democracy. He feared Hamilton's business policies would create a wealthy elite and duplicate the European social order in which every man was "either hammer or anvil."[128]

The two also clashed over relations with France. Hamilton persuaded Washington to follow a policy of neutrality toward Great Britain and France when they went to war, much to the chagrin of Jefferson, who loved France and backed the French Revolution.

A Character Sketch

William Leigh Pierce of Georgia, who briefly attended the Constitutional Convention but did not sign the finished document, wrote a series of character sketches of fellow delegates. They were not published until a century after he died in 1789. This portrait is taken from a biography of Hamilton by John F. Roche.

"Col. Hamilton is deservedly celebrated for his talents. He is a practitioner of the law, and reputed to be a finished scholar. To a clear and strong judgment he unites the ornaments of fancy, and while he is able, convincing, and engaging in his eloquence, the heart and head sympathize in approving him. Yet there is something too feeble in his voice to be equal to the strains of oratory. It is my opinion that he is rather a convincing speaker than a blazing orator.

Col. Hamilton requires time to think—he enquires into every part of his subject with the searchings of philosophy, and when he comes forward he comes highly charged with interesting matter. There is no skirmishing over the surface of a subject with him, he must sink to the bottom to see what foundation it rests on. His language is not always equal, sometimes didactic . . . at others light and tripping. His eloquence [does not] trifle with the senses, but he rambles just enough to strike and keep up the attention.

He is about 33 years old, of small stature, and lean. His manners are tinctured with stiffness, and sometimes with a degree of vanity that is highly disagreeable."

But years later even Jefferson, who quit his post under Washington partly out of frustration because Hamilton kept winning their battles, admitted that Hamilton had built well for the future. "We can pay off his debts in 15 years," he admitted ruefully, "but we can never get rid of his financial system."[129]

The Reynolds Affairs

Hamilton had many other political enemies besides Jefferson. When he advocated paying off state debts along with national debts and then creating a national bank, he was accused of trying to personally profit from his ideas. Though Congress officially investigated him in March 1791, his opponents were never able to prove Hamilton made even a dime illegally.

Hamilton, however, like Jefferson, got into trouble over a scandalous affair. In 1791 Hamilton became involved with a married woman named Maria Reynolds. Her husband, James Reynolds, blackmailed Hamilton, who paid eleven hundred dollars to keep the adultery secret.

In December 1792 future president James Monroe and two other congressmen met with Hamilton to discuss rumors that he had been involved in illegal business transactions with Reynolds, a speculator and swindler. The specific allegations were that the two had tried to profit by cheaply buying up debts the government owed to war veterans. Hamilton confessed that the only financial transactions between them had been blackmail he paid because of his affair with Reynolds's wife. Hamilton's admission cleared his name with the congressmen, who promised to keep the scandalous details secret.

In 1797, however, James T. Callender, the same journalist who revealed Jefferson's affair with Sally Hemings, printed the allegations concerning Hamilton and Reynolds. To clear himself, Hamilton published a pamphlet about his affair, admitting, "My real crime is an amorous connection with his wife."[130] Hamilton believed it was better to be considered a sexual cheat than a financial thief.

Return to Private Life

By the time the affair was made public, Hamilton had been in private life for two years. He had returned to his law practice in New York City in 1795 because government service, which did not pay very well, had put him on the edge of poverty. "I am not worth exceeding five hundred dollars in the world," Hamilton lamented in a self-pitying letter at the time. "My slender fortune and the best years of my life have been devoted to the service of my adopted country; a rising family hath its claims."[131]

However, Hamilton remained active in politics while rebuilding his law practice and his fortune. He continued to advise Washington and helped him write his famous farewell address. In 1797, when France and the United States appeared headed for war, Congress asked Washington to head a new army. He consented, but only if Hamilton would have actual command of the troops. Hamilton jumped at the chance for more personal glory and was named a senior major general. But when no fighting materialized except for minor naval clashes, the army was disbanded in June 1800; Washington and Hamilton returned to private life without ever having gone to war.

It was during this period that Hamilton earned the enmity of Aaron Burr, who was elected vice president under Jefferson in 1800. When the two candidates had tied for president, Hamilton threw his support to Jefferson because he believed Burr was a danger to the nation. In the 1804 election for governor of New York, Hamilton again angered Burr by helping to deny Burr the Republican nomination. Hamilton claimed publicly that Burr was "a dangerous man" and added he had "a still more despicable opinion"[132] of Burr he would not reveal publicly.

A Duel to the Death

Their quarrel escalated, and on June 18 Burr demanded a retraction of Hamilton's accusations. When Hamilton refused, Burr challenged him to a duel. Hamilton accepted even though he opposed the illegal act of dueling and was still mourning the death of his son, Philip, who was killed in a duel three years earlier while defending his father's honor. When the two met on July 11 in Weehawken, New Jersey, Burr's first shot struck Hamilton, hitting a rib and driving through his liver and diaphragm before lodging in his spine. Hamilton died the next day.

Before the duel, Hamilton had written to his wife:

> This letter, my dear Eliza, will not be delivered to you unless I shall have first terminated my earthly career to begin, I hope, a happy immortality. If it had been possible for me to have avoided the interview, my love for you and my precious children would have been alone a decisive motive. But it was not possible without sacrifices which would have rendered me unworthy of your esteem. I cherish the sweet hope of meeting you in a better world.[133]

Aaron Burr fatally shoots Alexander Hamilton. Their illegal duel July 11, 1804, in Weehawken, New Jersey, was the result of political quarrels between two of American history's most famous early figures.

Like Jefferson, his greatest political enemy, Hamilton died heavily in debt. And like John Adams, another foe, Hamilton died believing he deserved more recognition for his contributions to the founding of a new nation. Several years before his death, Hamilton had written to a friend:

> Perhaps no man in the United States has done more for the present Constitution than myself and contrary to all anticipations of its fate, as you know from the very beginning, I am still laboring to prop the frail and worthless fabric. Yet I have the murmurs of its friends no less than the curses of its foes for my reward. Every day proves to me more and more, that this America was not made for me.[134]

Clearly, however, Hamilton helped make "this America" and he is honored today as one of its greatest historical figures.

CHAPTER 6

John Adams: The Puritan Rebel

John Adams was a man of many accomplishments: a successful lawyer, a thinking man's revolutionary whose legalistic arguments persuaded many Americans that the cause of independence was just, a foreign diplomat, the nation's first vice president, and its second president. Yet Adams once wrote, "If I were to live over my life again, I would be a shoemaker rather than a statesman."[135]

Adams surely derived less joy and satisfaction from creating a new nation than any other founder; although he valued what he helped build (Adams was a passionate believer in the new nation that granted its citizens more rights and freedom than any in history), he was childishly angry that he never received enough personal glory. At key moments in his career, Adams was fated to be overshadowed by others.

Although one of Boston's leading revolutionaries, his cousin Samuel Adams was better liked and initially more famous; for many years John was referred to as "the other Adams." Adams supervised the selection of George Washington as commander in chief only to envy him when he rode off to glory. Adams ordered Jefferson to write the Declaration of Independence but regretted it when the assignment made Jefferson famous. As a diplomat in Europe, Adams was secondary to Benjamin Franklin. A mere shadow figure as vice president under Washington, when Adams was finally elected president he struggled through a rocky four years. Adams was then defeated for reelection by Jefferson, who once had been a friend but was now a political nemesis.

His envy of the accolades other founders reaped by their efforts made Adams bitter, as in this sarcastic assessment he once penned:

> The history of our revolution will be one continued lye. The essence of the whole will be that Dr. Franklin's electrical rod smote the earth and out sprung General Wash-

ington. That Franklin enlivened him with his rod—and thence forward these two conducted all the policy, negotiations, legislatures, and war.[136]

Growing Up

A fifth-generation American, Adams was born on October 19, 1735, in Braintree (now Quincy), Massachusetts. John Adams Sr., a shoemaker and local official, had married Susanna Boylston, the daughter of a prominent, wealthy family. As a youngster Adams enjoyed farm chores and hunting, but his father wanted him to become a minister. He learned to read at age six, went to Free Latin School two years later, and at age fifteen entered what is now Harvard University, graduating four years later fourteenth in a class of twenty-five.

In what was supposed to be a brief interlude before becoming a minister, Adams began teaching grammar school in Worcester. But when Adams began worrying that he would "live and die an ignorant, obscure fellow,"[137] his ego led him to switch career paths and decide to become a lawyer, the profession of several other founders.

Although Adams decided on law because he believed that position offered him a chance at fame, which he desperately sought throughout his life, he realized even then that his vanity was a character flaw. While teaching in Worcester, Adams wrote in his diary, "Oh! that I could swear out of my mind every mean and base affectation, conquer my natural pride and self conceit, expect no more deference from my fellows than I deserve, acquire that meekness, and humility, which are the sure marks and characters of a great and generous soul."[138] Conquering his pride was something Adams would fail at throughout his life. Alexander Hamilton once accused Adams of having "disgusting egotism."[139]

A "Brace of Adamses"

Admitted to the Boston bar in 1758, Adams lived in Braintree and rode from town to town trying cases and winning clients as he proved his courtroom skill. Samuel Adams, who was more volatile and fiery than John, was an early convert to the patriot cause. John was won over to the cause in 1761 after listening to lawyer and statesman James Otis argue eloquently that British interference in Massachusetts government was illegal.

When the British Parliament passed the Stamp Act in 1765, Samuel and John Adams teamed up to oppose it: Sam organized the militant Sons of Liberty while John wrote a series of resolutions condemning the tax that were adopted by Braintree and other Massachusetts towns. They were such an effective pair that in 1770, when both were elected to the Massachusetts legislature, Governor William Shirley grumbled, "Where this brace of Adamses comes from, I know not."[140]

In the early years of the Revolution Samuel Adams (pictured) was more well known than his cousin, John Adams.

In the famous Braintree Instructions, which John Adams wrote for his hometown, he predicted the Stamp Act would "drain the country of its cash, strip multitudes of all their property, and reduce them to absolutely beggary." He argued that the tax was inconsistent not only with the spirit of British common law but also "the essential fundamental principles of the British Constitution."[141]

This and other forceful political essays appeared in newspapers, placing Adams in the front ranks of the emerging rebellion. One reason why Adams was able to forge bold new ideas was because he never stopped learning. Historian Richard B. Morris explains that Adams continued to educate himself his entire life:

> As with most of the Founding Fathers, Adams was largely self-educated. In the main what he learned was from books, he was an omnivorous reader and, from early manhood, an indefatigable book collector. Ten years of law practice had given him [the means] to build a substantial library. By 1771 he was recklessly ordering from London "every book and pamphlet of reputation upon the subjects of law and government as soon as it comes out." With such a blanket order to his booksellers, one can understand why three years later he had already spent 400 pounds sterling, "an estate in books," and he never could curb this one extravagance. His library of some three thousand titles represented an extraordinary range of interests.[142]

The Boston Massacre

Adams played a unique role in the Boston Massacre by agreeing to defend British soldiers involved in the incident despite his patriot sentiments. Adams did this because he disliked the violent tactics the Sons of Liberty had used to harass the soldiers and because he believed they deserved a fair trial. "Counsel," he said, "ought to be the very last thing that an accused man should [lack] in a free country."[143]

The night of March 5, 1770, was clear and cold, a foot of new snow covering the ground. The infamous massacre began when a sentry at Boston's custom house struck a barber's apprentice with his musket after the youth taunted him, claiming the soldier's commanding officer had failed to pay his barber bills. Church bells tolled in alarm, rallying Sons of Liberty and others to the scene as almost four hundred angry patriots besieged the lone soldier.

Captain Thomas Preston led seven other soldiers to the beleagured sentry's aid only to be pelted by rocks, snowballs, oyster shells, and street debris thrown by angry patriots. "Kill the lobsters, kill them!" some in the crowd raged while others shouted, "You dare not fire!"[144] When one panicky soldier did shoot, the others unleashed a deadly volley that killed five men, who were considered the first casualties of the American Revolution.

One of the protest leaders was Crispus Attucks, a runaway slave who worked on the docks in Boston and was well known in the city. Attucks was a big man, strongly built, and fierce despite his fifty-one years. Part Natick Indian—*Attucks* means "deer" in the Natick language—he was an escaped slave who sometimes used the name Michael Johnson. When Attucks escaped, the Massachusetts man who owned him ran a newspaper advertisement

Crispus Attucks, the African American who was one of the Revolution's first heroes, is the first to die in the Boston Massacre.

seeking his return and describing him as "a mulatto fellow, about 27 years of age, named Crispus, 6-feet-2-inches high, short, curl'd hair, his knees nearer together than common."[145]

While defending soldiers in the Boston Massacre, Adams claimed that Attucks had decided "to be the hero of the night, and to lead this army with banners, to form them in the first place in Dock Square, and march them up to King Street with their clubs." Adams also said Attucks was so ferocious in appearance that his "very looks was enough to terrify any person."[146] Attucks was the first patriot shot, after bravely grabbing a bayonet protruding from the end of a British musket.

Charging "there was a mob in Boston on the fifth of March that attacked a party of soldiers,"[147] Adams won acquittal for Pre-

The Boston Massacre

Many people wonder how John Adams, a patriot, could have defended the British soldiers charged in the Boston Massacre. But in Liberty! The American Revolution, *author Thomas Fleming explains that Adams may have defended them to benefit the patriot cause.*

"From a popular leader of the Sons of Liberty, Adams became a scorned man. Rocks were flung through his windows and boys jeered him in the streets. He was not helped by his cousin Samuel's tactics. At a Boston town meeting, 3,000 roaring Sons of Liberty demanded the immediate removal of the troops from Boston. John Adams stubbornly persevered in the soldiers' defense. Deploying his witnesses with a nice combination of bluntness and finesse, Adams convincingly demonstrated that the soldiers had acted in self-defense against a riotous mob. . . . He accomplished this feat without using any evidence that might have embarrassed individual Sons of Liberty, in particular Samuel Adams.

Unquestionably [Adams] won friends in England and in other colonies by demonstrating that Massachusetts upheld the rule of law. In Boston Samuel Adams did not seem to agree. He denounced the juries' verdicts and the defense argument in a series of scathing articles in *The Boston Gazette*. Privately, his friendship with John Adams became even more intimate. It would seem more than likely that Samuel Adams realized that without John Adams at the defense table, the evidence gathered on behalf of the British soldiers might have sent him and other members of the Liberty party to London under arrest for treason. The trials helped John convince Samuel that the Sons of Liberty's policy of violence was almost out of control and must be tempered henceforth."

ston, who was tried separately from the other soldiers. He argued successfully that Preston and the others acted in self-defense. In the second trial, only two soldiers were found guilty of manslaughter. They got off lightly by being branded on the thumb and discharged.

For the rest of his life, Adams claimed that his defense of the redcoats was "one of the best pieces of service I ever rendered my country."[148] He did not present any information to incriminate individual members of the "mob," including his cousin Sam; thus, the trial did not undermine the Sons of Liberty or his own revolutionary standing.

Revolutionary, Family Man

Adams was an important figure in the revolutionary movement in Massachusetts, the major hotbed of rebellion in the colonies. As a legislator, Adams fought against British interference in colonial affairs, his reputation growing from the forceful essays he wrote that claimed England had no legal or moral right to govern the colonies. In one article, which was signed "Novanglus" (Latin for "New England"), he proclaimed "America is not any part of the British realm" and that Americans would fight English repression: "We will not stand still to be butchered. We will defend our lives as long as providence shall enable us."[149]

In 1768 Adams moved his family to Boston. Four years earlier he had married Abigail Smith, a woman who was his intellectual and psychological equal though a decade younger. The marriage lasted fifty-four years and produced five children; Adams lived to see his oldest son, John Quincy Adams, elected the nation's sixth president in 1825.

Abigail was a strong woman, unafraid to speak her mind or stand up to her husband. When they first met, Adams commented that the book she was reading, *Human Understanding* by philosopher John Locke, was too difficult "for such a little head." She replied, "You think so? Yet girls too may have their curiosity."[150] Abigail was a strong partner and even more radical than her husband, whom she often accused of being too cautious in seeking independence. John once told her, "You are fiery as a young grenadier, Abby."[151]

As a delegate to the Continental Congress, Adams played a key role in two of the most important actions of the Revolutionary War. The first was to win approval of Washington as head of the Continental army and the second to command Jefferson to write the Declaration of Independence. Jefferson's resulting fame, however, fractured their friendship for many years. Adams was so envious that in his old age he spitefully labeled the historic document a "juvenile declamation" and claimed, "The Declaration of Independence I always considered as a theatrical show. Jefferson ran away with all the stage effect . . . and all the glory of it."[152]

Jefferson was much kinder in assessing Adams, who played a major role in convincing delegates to declare independence. "John Adams was our Colossus on the floor," said Jefferson. "He was not graceful nor elegant, nor remarkably fluent" but he had "a power of thought and expression that moved us from our seats."[153]

Adams wrongly predicted that July 2, the day Congress approved Richard Henry Lee's independence resolution, and not July 4 would be celebrated as the birth of America:

> The second day of July 1776 will be the most memorable [day] in the history of America. I am apt to believe that it will be celebrated by succeeding generations as the great anniversary festival. It ought to be solemnized with pomp, and parade, with shows, games, sports, bells, bonfires, and illuminations, from one end of the colonies to the other, from this time forward forevermore.[154]

Instead, America celebrates July 4, adding to the honor and glory Jefferson earned and Adams gave away.

Diplomat

Benjamin Franklin once said Adams was "always an honest man, often a wise one, but sometimes, and in some things, absolutely out of his sense."[155] There was no love lost between the two, but they had to work together in 1778 when Adams was assigned to France as a diplomat. Adams envied Franklin's fame and disliked his fun-loving lifestyle, which offended Adams's own puritanical sense of morality.

In 1785, when Adams became the first U.S. ambassador to Great Britain, Jonathan Sewall, a former royal official in Massachusetts who had once tried to persuade Adams to abandon the patriot cause, said Adams was an odd choice as diplomat:

> He was as honest a lawyer as ever broke bread but he is not qualified, by nature or education, to shine in courts. His abilities are undoubtedly equal to the mechanical parts of his business as ambassador, but this is not enough. He cannot dance, drink, game, flatter, promise, dress, swear with the gentlemen and talk small talk and flirt with the ladies. In short, he has none of the essential arts or ornaments which constitute a courtier.[156]

A Letter from Abigail Adams

Abigail Adams was a rarity for her time, a woman with education who was not afraid to speak out on social issues. Because women in the colonial period were not admitted to schools of higher education, Abigail was self-educated and had read widely in history and other subjects; her husband considered her an intellectual equal. She was also one of the earliest recorded feminists in U.S. history.

On March 31, 1776, while John was in Philadelphia attending the Continental Congress, Abigail wrote to her husband asking him to make sure that women, as well as men, would be able to enjoy the independence for which Americans were fighting. On April 14 John answered with a letter of his own, but his comments were far from sympathetic and treated the subject in a joking manner. The following excerpts of the letters are taken from The American Reader: Words That Moved a Nation.

"ABIGAIL: I desire you would remember the ladies, and be more generous and favorable to them than your ancestors. Do not put such unlimited power into the hands of the husbands. Remember all men would be tyrants if they could. If particular care and attention is not paid to the ladies we are determined to foment a rebellion, and will not hold ourselves bound by any laws in which we have no voice, or representation. That your sex are naturally tyrannical is a truth so thoroughly established as to admit of no dispute, but such of you as which to be happy willingly give up the harsh title of master for the more tender and endearing one of friend.

JOHN: Depend upon it. We know better than to repeal our masculine systems. Altho they are in full force, you know they are little more than theory. We dare not exert our power in its full latitude. We are obliged to go fair, and softly, and in practice you know we are the subjects. We have only the name of masters, and rather than give up this, which would compleatly subject us to the despotism of the petticoat, I hope General Washington, and all our brave heroes would fight."

Abigail Adams equaled her husband, John, both in intellect and her fierce desire for freedom from Great Britain.

The refusal of King George III to compromise with colonists was a major factor in causing the American Revolution.

But Adams established relations with Holland, helped work out the peace treaty that ended the Revolutionary War, and charmed even King George III when he met him by offering his country's "best wishes for your Majesty's health and for that of your royal family." His gracious comments so pleased the king that George commented, "I am very glad the choice has fallen on you to be minister."[157]

Vice President

Adams returned home in 1788 to finally gain some of the recognition he craved by being elected vice president. He served two terms under Washington, but even this high post did not satisfy him.

Many precedents, roles, and traditions for the federal government and its officials were set during Washington's first term. Unfortunately for Adams, Washington did not like him very much and did not consult him when making important decisions, inviting him to only two or three cabinet meetings in eight years. Since they were not close, Adams spent most of his time in the Senate chambers presiding over that body.

Without real power and shut out from decision making, the unhappy Adams called the vice presidency "the most insignificant office that ever the invention of man contrived or his imagination conceived."[158] Adams thus helped shape the post for all time, and his lament has been shared by every vice president since.

It was during his vice presidency that the short, plump Adams was first called "His Rotundity," a nickname that stemmed not only from his physique but also from his preference for pomp and ceremony. In trying to establish traditions for the office of president, Adams and some others wanted to ape the dramatic ceremonies and titles of European royalty, which Jefferson and others despised for officials in a democratic society. Adams, who as a diplomat in Europe had grown to appreciate the pageantry of royalty, argued that if Washington was not given the title "Majesty," he would be scorned in Europe. Luckily, his suggestion was rejected.

President Adams

In 1796 Adams was elected president over Jefferson: At last he was the most important man in the United States. But his four years as chief executive were troubled ones. During his term the Federalist Party he headed fell apart; he had to contend with a political foe, Jefferson, as vice president; and he was increasingly criticized by both Federalists and Republicans. Problems with France, once an ally but now an enemy after undergoing its own revolution, dominated his unhappy term.

France, at war again with Great Britain, was upset about President Washington's pro-British policies. After 1794 France began treating American ships carrying goods to Britain as enemy ships, seizing them and confiscating cargo. In 1797 Adams sent a bipartisan commission to France to make peace, however, three French officials asked for a bribe in what became known as the XYZ Affair: Its name came from the letters of the alphabet Adams used to refer to the French diplomats. The incident infuriated Hamilton and his Federalist followers, who demanded that Adams declare war on France. But Adams bravely declined, sending another group of diplomats who resolved the problems and averted war.

Federalists in Congress then passed the Alien and Sedition Acts, which restricted French radicals now living in America, who they feared would support the Republicans, and made it illegal for Republican newspapers to criticize the government. Adams was uncomfortable with the laws but did not veto them, an act that tarnished his reputation because they were unfair and betrayed the principles of liberty that are the nation's foundation.

In 1800 Adams became the first president to lose his bid for reelection when Jefferson triumphed. A bitter, broken man, Adams left Washington in the early hours on the day Jefferson was inaugurated—he could not bear to watch his successor sworn in as president.

A strong sense of morality gave John Adams the drive to fight for what he believed was right, no matter what the odds. But his personality was flawed by jealousy and a disturbing desire for personal glory.

His Final Years

Adams lived another twenty-five years as an unhappy ex-president who gradually resigned himself to what he believed was a lack of recognition for his service to his country. Adams once commented that he took part in the American Revolution because, "I was borne along by an irresistible sense of duty."[159] That moral sense led him to accomplish great things for his country, but his own inner flaws alienated many people, made him unhappy even with some of his successes, and almost always led him to envy the accolades and fame granted his fellow founders.

In addition to watching the rise of his son to the presidency, one of his greatest joys was to renew his friendship with Jefferson. In 1812, partly at the urging of his wife, Adams wrote to Jefferson. For the next fourteen years, they exchanged many letters. In one of the great ironies of history, they both died on July 4, 1826, the fiftieth anniversary of the passage of the Declaration of Independence, the event that made Jefferson famous and Adams supremely envious for having passed up the opportunity to write the historic document.

Adams, who was sick and knew he was dying, had lapsed into a coma that day but awoke at about 1 P.M. His last words were, "Thomas Jefferson survives."[160] Adams died at about sunset, not knowing that Jefferson had died a few hours earlier.

It Took Many to Make a Nation

The five historical figures whose lives are detailed in this book continue to be revered for their part in founding the United States of America. Enduring symbols of the courage, spirit, and wisdom that fueled the American Revolution and established a new, more just system of government, they are honored today in many ways, from U.S. currency that bears their likeness to holidays such as the Fourth of July that honor their accomplishments.

But unlike John Adams and Alexander Hamilton, who at times crabbily complained they had not received enough credit for their efforts, Benjamin Franklin wisely knew that he and other founders played only a small part in creating a new nation. When a French official praised Franklin, saying he had "snatched the lightning from the sky and the scepter from the tyrants" for overthrowing British rule, the one-time printer's apprentice quickly rejected the grandiose compliment: "It ascribes too much to me—the Revolution was the work of many able and brave men, wherein it is sufficient honor for me if I am allowed a small share [of honor]."[161] Franklin knew that millions of Americans, men and women alike, had endured great hardships and made tremendous sacrifices to defeat Great Britain in the Revolutionary War and to establish a new nation.

Other Heroes and Heroines

It is generally believed that 25,324 Americans died in the Revolutionary War, with almost 10,000 falling to illnesses like smallpox and dysentery in military camps such as Valley Forge while another 8,500 died while being held as prisoners of war. The figures, however, are considered conservative. There are also no solid records for the number of civilians who died, which means the overall death toll is much higher.

Although only men were allowed to become soldiers during the Revolutionary War, some patriotic women did fight for their country. African American Deborah Gannett dressed in men's clothing and enlisted in the Fourth Massachusetts regiment as Robert Shirtliffe. She served for nearly eighteen months and was wounded twice—by a sword cut on the side of her head and a bullet wound to the shoulder.

Hundreds of women also followed their husbands to war and served as nurses, washerwomen, and cooks; most simply had no other way to support themselves while their husbands were at war. Some of these women wound up fighting alongside their mates in battlefield emergencies. During the war, women also served as spies.

Crispus Attucks was not the only African American hero of the Revolution. About five thousand African Americans served in the Continental army, some in all-black regiments, fighting in every battle from Lexington to Yorktown. Many were slaves who enlisted to earn their freedom, fighting for their own independence as well as that of their country's.

Other heroes included John Paul Jones, who became America's first naval hero after a series of daring raids on the British coast; Paul Revere, the Boston silversmith whose midnight ride warned patriots that the British were marching to Concord and helped rally minutemen to resist their advance; and James Madison, often called "the Father of the Constitution" for contributions he made in framing the important document. That was an accolade, however, the Virginia-born fourth president of the United States would not accept. "You give me credit," Madison once said, "to which I have no claim, in calling me '*the* writer of the Constitution of the United States.' This was not the offspring of a single brain. It ought to be regarded as the work of many heads and many hands."[162]

Historian Page Smith concurs: "The American Revolution was not made by a small group of radical intellectuals; it was formed in the consciousness of Americans in every colony and every walk of life, perhaps even more strongly in the plain people of the colonies than among their leaders."[163]

Understanding History

To truly understand history, whether it is that of America or the entire world, one must examine the human factors that drive key events. Thus, the easiest way to understand the American

Revolution is to reduce it to the human motivation that drove colonists to defy what was then the world's most powerful nation.

Ironically, it was a Captain Evelyn, a British officer serving in Boston, who most succinctly summed up the *real* cause of the Revolution in a letter to his father in February 1775. It was "the nature of mankind," he wrote, that was leading Americans to defy Great Britain and demand their independence: "I think that it proceeds from a new nation, feeling itself wealthy, populous, and strong; and that [colonists], being impatient of restraint, are struggling to throw off the dependency which is so irksome to them."[164]

Adopted in 1788, the Constitution became a blueprint for greatness. It united the colonies and in the next two centuries enabled a weak, fledgling nation to become the strongest the world had ever seen.

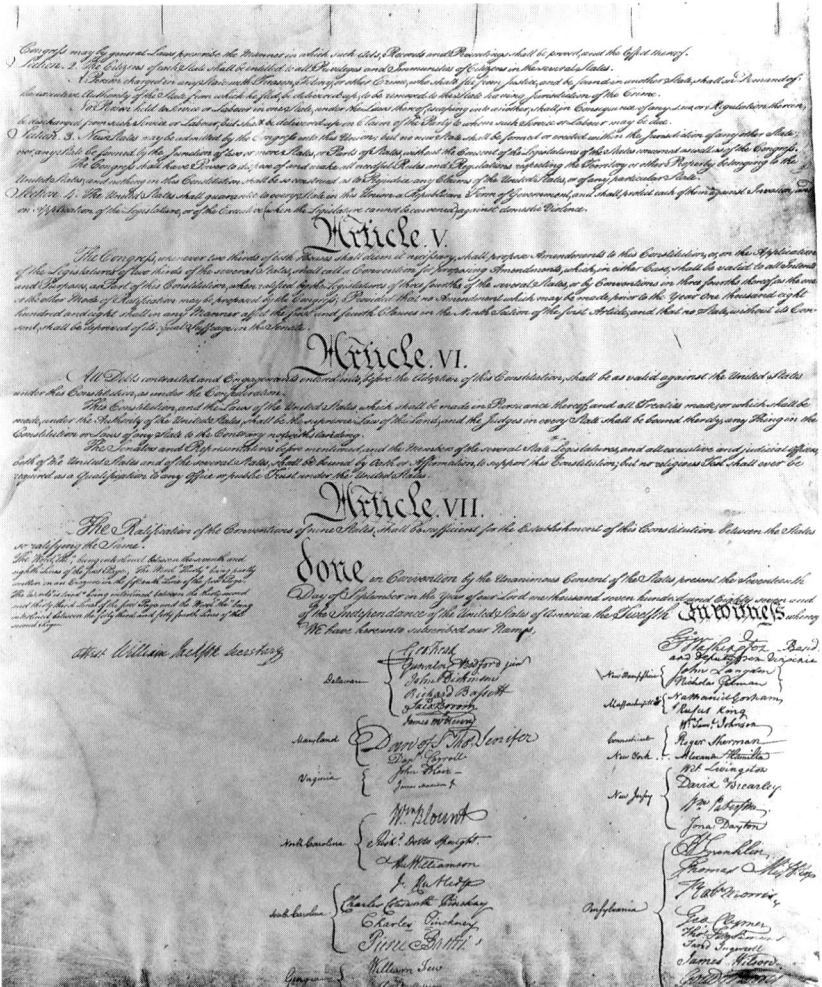

Like an adult child yearning for independence from his or her parents, Americans were simply ready to make their own way in the world. The cause of the American Revolution was as simple as that. Yet without leaders like George Washington, Benjamin Franklin, Thomas Jefferson, Alexander Hamilton, and John Adams to properly harness the energy and drive resulting from this basic human emotion, the Revolution might have failed.

Thus, Americans will always owe an immense debt to these five founders.

NOTES

Introduction: Five Who Changed History

1. Quoted in Richard D. Heffner, *A Documentary History of the United States*. Bloomington: Indiana University Press, 1952, p. 9.

2. Page Smith, *Jefferson: A Revealing Biography*. New York: American Heritage, 1976, p. 306.

Chapter 1: The American Revolution: Two Revolutions in One

3. Quoted in Thomas Fleming, *Liberty! The American Revolution*. New York: Penguin, 1998, p. 355.

4. Quoted in Richard B. Morris, *Seven Who Shaped Our Destiny: The Founding Fathers as Revolutionaries*. New York: Harper & Row, 1973, p. 79.

5. Quoted in Diane Ravitch, ed., *The American Reader: Words That Moved a Nation*. New York: HarperCollins, 1990, p. 3.

6. Winthrop D. Jordan, Miriam Greenblatt, and John S. Bowes, *The Americans: The History of a People and a Nation*. Evanston, IL: McDougal, Littell, 1985, p. 76.

7. John A. Garraty with Robert A. McCaughey, *The American Nation: A History of the United States to 1877*, vol. 1, 7th ed. New York: HarperCollins, 1991, p. 37.

8. Quoted in Robert C. Baron, ed., *Soul of America: Documenting Our Past, 1492–1974*. Golden, CO: Fulcrum, 1989, p. 22.

9. Quoted in Garraty and McCaughey, *The American Nation*, p. 88.

10. Page Smith, *A New Age Now Begins: A People's History of the American Revolution*, vol. 1. New York: McGraw-Hill, 1976, p. 251.

11. Quoted in Garraty and McCaughey, *The American Nation*, p. 93.

12. Quoted in Fleming, *Liberty!* p. 68.

13. Quoted in Albert Marrin, *The War for Independence: The Story of the American Revolution*. New York: Atheneum, 1988, p. 36.

14. Quoted in Garraty and McCaughey, *The American Nation*, p. 102.

15. Quoted in Richard B. Morris, *The Life History of the United States*, vol. 2, *1775–1789: The Making of a Nation*. New York: Time-Life Books, 1963, p. 9.

16. Quoted in Smith, *A New Age Now Begins*, vol. 1, p. 479.

17. Quoted in Marrin, *The War for Independence*, p. 1.

18. Quoted in Michael Kraus, *The United States to 1865*. Ann Arbor: University of Michigan Press, 1969, p. 216.

19. Fleming, *Liberty!* p. 327.

20. Quoted in Smith, *A New Age Now Begins*, vol. 2, p. 1,717.

21. Quoted in Jordan, Greenblatt, and Bowes, *The Americans*, p. 128.

22. Quoted in National Archives and Records Administration, "The Declaration of Independence: A Transcription." www.nara.gov/exhall/charters/declaration/declaration.html.

23. Quoted in Jordan, Greenblatt, and Bowes, *The Americans*, p. 161.

24. Smith, *A New Age Now Begins*, vol. 2, p. 1,817.

Chapter 2: George Washington: Father of His Country

25. Quoted in Paul F. Boller Jr., *Presidential Anecdotes*. New York: Oxford University Press, 1981, p. 7.

26. Quoted in Garraty and McCaughey, *The American Nation*, p. 133.

27. Quoted in David C. Whitney, *The American Presidents*. Garden City, NY: Doubleday, 1978, p. 5.

28. Willard Sterne Randall, *George Washington: A Life*. New York: Henry Holt, 1997, p. 49.

29. Quoted in Zachary Kent, *Encyclopedia of Presidents: George Washington*. Chicago: Childrens Press, 1986, p. 22.

30. Quoted in Randall, *George Washington*, p. 101.

31. Quoted in Whitney, *The American Presidents*, p. 7.

32. Quoted in Randall, *George Washington*, p. 137.

33. Quoted in Randall, *George Washington*, p. 236.

34. Quoted in Catherine Drinker Bowen, *John Adams and the American Revolution*. Boston: Little, Brown, 1950, p. 533.

35. Marrin, *The War for Independence*, p. 68.

36. Quoted in Whitney, *The American Presidents*, p. 10.

37. Page Smith, *A New Age Now Begins*, vol. 1, p. 824.

38. Quoted in Randall, *George Washington*, p. 327.

39. Quoted in Marrin, *The War for Independence*, p. 116.

40. Quoted in Marrin, *The War for Independence*, p. 144.

41. Quoted in Marrin, *The War for Independence*, p. 264.

42. Quoted in Randall, *George Washington*, p. 396.

43. Quoted in Charles W. Meister, *The Founding Fathers*. Jefferson, NC: McFarland, 1987, p. 333.

44. Quoted in Fleming, *Liberty!* p. 358.

45. Quoted in Fleming, *Liberty!* p. 360.

46. Quoted in Boller, *Presidential Anecdotes*, p. 14.

47. Quoted in Margaret L. Coit, *The Life History of the United States*, vol. 3, *1789–1829: The Growing Years*. New York: Time-Life Books, 1963, p. 7.

48. Quoted in Kent, *Encyclopedia of Presidents*, p. 10.

49. Quoted in Wendie C. Old, *George Washington*. Springfield, NJ: Enslow, 1997, p. 87.

50. Quoted in Coit, *The Life History of the United States*, vol. 3, p. 12.

51. Quoted in Randall, *George Washington*, p. 502.

Chapter 3: Benjamin Franklin: The Most Famous Colonial

52. Alfred Tamarin, ed., *Benjamin Franklin: An Autobiographical Portrait*. London: Macmillan, 1969, p. v.

53. Quoted in James Daugherty, *Poor Richard*. New York: The Viking Press, 1946, p. 15.

54. Quoted in Tamarin, *Benjamin Franklin*, p. 5.

55. Quoted in Tamarin, *Benjamin Franklin*, p. 7.

56. Garraty and McCaughey, *The American Nation*, p. 68.

57. Quoted in Daugherty, *Poor Richard*, p. 23.

58. Ronald W. Clark, *Benjamin Franklin: A Biography*. New York: Random House, 1983, p. 24.

59. Quoted in Ravitch, *The American Reader*, p. 4.

60. Morris, *Seven Who Shaped Our Destiny*, p. 7.

61. Quoted in Clark, *Benjamin Franklin*, p. 54.

62. Quoted in Meister, *The Founding Fathers*, p. 79.

63. Quoted in Tamarin, *Benjamin Franklin*, p. 97.

64. Quoted in Clark, *Benjamin Franklin*, pp. 192–93.

65. Quoted in Daugherty, *Poor Richard*, p. 112.

66. Quoted in Tamarin, *Benjamin Franklin*, p. 200.

67. Quoted in Clark, *Benjamin Franklin*, p. 286.

68. Quoted in Meister, *The Founding Fathers*, p. 90.

69. Quoted in Clark, *Benjamin Franklin*, p. 356.

70. Quoted in Daugherty, *Poor Richard*, p. 143.

71. Fleming, *Liberty!* p. 361.

72. Quoted in Baron, *Soul of America*, p. 99.

73. Quoted in Baron, *Soul of America*, p. 100.

74. Quoted in Meister, *The Founding Fathers*, p. 93.

75. Quoted in Clark, *Benjamin Franklin*, p. 16.

Chapter 4: Thomas Jefferson: Author of the Declaration of Independence

76. Quoted in Bill Adler, ed., *The Kennedy Wit*. New York: Citadel, 1964, p. 43.

77. Don Nardo, *Thomas Jefferson*. San Diego: Lucent Books, 1993, p. 12.

78. Quoted in Nardo, *Thomas Jefferson*, p. 15.

79. Quoted in Fawn M. Brodie, *Thomas Jefferson: An Intimate History*. New York: W. W. Norton, 1974, p. 39.

80. Quoted in Smith, *Jefferson*, p. 15.

81. Quoted in Nardo, *Thomas Jefferson*, p. 2.

82. Smith, *Jefferson*, p. 37.

83. Quoted in Brodie, *Thomas Jefferson*, p. 80.

84. Quoted in Nardo, *Thomas Jefferson*, p. 33.

85. Quoted in Smith, *Jefferson*, p. 93.

86. Quoted in National Archives and Records Administration, "The Declaration of Independence."

87. Quoted in Garraty and McCaughey, *The American Nation*, p. 112.

88. Quoted in Stuart Gerry Brown, *Thomas Jefferson*. New York: Washington Square, 1966, p. 36.

89. Quoted in Smith, *Jefferson*, p. 106.

90. Quoted in Brodie, *Thomas Jefferson,* p. 228.

91. Eugene A. Foster et al., "Jefferson Fathered Slave's Last Child," *Nature,* November 1998, p. 27.

92. Quoted in Brodie, *Thomas Jefferson,* pp. 91, 423.

93. Quoted in Brown, *Thomas Jefferson,* p. 20.

94. Smith, *Jefferson,* p. 93.

95. Coit, *The Life History of the United States,* vol. 3, p. 15.

96. Quoted in Smith, *Jefferson,* p. 239.

97. Quoted in Brodie, *Thomas Jefferson,* p. 282.

98. Quoted in Brodie, *Thomas Jefferson,* p. 243.

99. Quoted in Smith, *Jefferson,* p. 256.

100. Quoted in Ravitch, *The American Reader,* p. 42.

101. Quoted in Kraus, *The United States to 1865,* p. 301.

102. Quoted in Nardo, *Thomas Jefferson,* p. 83.

103 Quoted in Brodie, *Thomas Jefferson,* p. 349.

104. Quoted in Fleming, *Liberty!* p. 383.

Chapter 5: Alexander Hamilton: America's Financial Genius

105. Quoted in Morris, *Seven Who Shaped Our Destiny,* p. 221.

106. Quoted in Randall, *George Washington,* p. 457.

107. Quoted in Meister, *The Founding Fathers,* p. 126.

108. Garraty and McCaughey, *The American Nation,* p. 152.

109. John F. Roche, *Illustrious Americans: Alexander Hamilton.* Morristown, NJ: Silver Burdett, 1967, p. 10.

110. Quoted in Morris, *Seven Who Shaped Our Destiny,* p. 223.

111. Quoted in Nathan Schachner, *Alexander Hamilton.* New York: D. Appleton-Century, 1946, p. 19.

112. Quoted in Schachner, *Alexander Hamilton,* p. 24.

113. Quoted in Schachner, *Alexander Hamilton,* p. 238.

114. Roche, *Illustrious Americans,* p. 9.

115. Quoted in Roche, *Illustrious Americans,* p. 22.

116. Quoted in Schachner, *Alexander Hamilton,* pp. 110–11.

117. Quoted in Schachner, *Alexander Hamilton,* p. 235.

118. Quoted in Roche, *Illustrious Americans,* p. 31.

119. Quoted in Baron, *Soul of America*, p. 87.

120. Schachner, *Alexander Hamilton*, p. 98.

121. Quoted in Morris, *Seven Who Shaped Our Destiny*, pp. 230–31.

122. Quoted in Robert Maynard Hutchins, ed., *American State Papers: The* Federalist. Chicago: Encyclopaedia Brittanica, 1952, p. 30.

123. Quoted in Hutchins, *American State Papers*, p. 259.

124. Quoted in Garraty and McCaughey, *The American Nation*, p. 154.

125. Quoted in Heffner, *A Documentary History of the United States*, p. 50.

126. Quoted in Morris, *The Life History of the United States*, vol. 2, p. 45.

127. Quoted in Schachner, *Alexander Hamilton*, p. 174.

128. Quoted in Kraus, *The United States to 1865*, p. 298.

129. Quoted in Roche, *Illustrious Americans*, p. 88.

130. Quoted in Morris, *Seven Who Shaped Our Destiny*, p. 235.

131. Quoted in Schachner, *Alexander Hamilton*, p. 300.

132. Quoted in Roche, *Illustrious Americans*, p. 86.

133. Quoted in Meister, *The Founding Fathers*, p. 139.

134. Quoted in Schachner, *Alexander Hamilton*, p. 409.

Chapter 6: John Adams: The Puritan Rebel

135. Quoted in Brodie, *Thomas Jefferson*, p. 335.

136. Quoted in Boller, *Presidential Anecdotes*, p. 26.

137. Quoted in Morris, *Seven Who Shaped Our Destiny*, p. 74.

138. Quoted in Peter Shaw, *The Character of John Adams*. Chapel Hill: University of North Carolina Press, 1976, p. 19.

139. Quoted in Coit, *The Life History of the United States*, vol. 3, p. 33.

140. Quoted in Bowen, *John Adams and the American Revolution*, p. 257.

141. Quoted in Morris, *Seven Who Shaped Our Destiny*, p. 93.

142. Morris, *Seven Who Shaped Our Destiny*, p. 81.

143. Quoted in Fleming, *Liberty!* p. 72.

144. Quoted in Marrin, *The War for Independence*, p. 29.

145. Quoted in Phillip T. Drotning, *Black Heroes in Our Nation's History: A Tribute to Those Who Helped Shape America*. New York: Cowles, 1969, p. 17.

146. Quoted in Drotning, *Black Heroes in Our Nation's History*, p. 17.

147. Quoted in Smith, *A New Age Now Begins*, vol. 1, p. 355.

148. Quoted in Fleming, *Liberty!* p. 73.

149. Quoted in Bowen, *John Adams and the American Revolution*, p. 513.

150. Quoted in Bowen, *John Adams and the American Revolution*, p. 185.

151. Quoted in Bowen, *John Adams and the American Revolution*, p. 291.

152. Quoted in Shaw, *The Character of John Adams*, p. 100.

153. Quoted in Shaw, *The Character of John Adams*, p. 98.

154. Quoted in Boller, *Presidential Anecdotes*, p. 30.

155. Quoted in Boller, *Presidential Anecdotes*, p. 26.

156. Quoted in Morris, *Seven Who Shaped Our Destiny*, p. 97.

157. Quoted in Fleming, *Liberty!* p. 349.

158. Quoted in Whitney, *The American Presidents*, p. 25.

159. Quoted in Morris, *Seven Who Shaped Our Destiny*, p. 77.

160. Quoted in Boller, *Presidential Anecdotes*, p. 27.

Epilogue: It Took Many to Make a Nation

161. Quoted in Daugherty, *Poor Richard*, p. 137.

162. Quoted in Meister, *The Founding Fathers*, p. 151.

163. Smith, *A New Age Now Begins*, vol. 2, p. 1,825.

164. Quoted in Kraus, *The United States to 1865*, p. 206.

1607
Jamestown, Virginia, the first permanent English colony, is founded on May 13 by more than one hundred colonists on the banks of the James River.

1619
The first slaves arrive in Virginia in August when a Dutch ship brings twenty blacks to Jamestown.

1620
Pilgrims reach Plymouth, Massachusetts, in December aboard the *Mayflower.*

1754
A battle on July 4 between French soldiers and George Washington's forces ignites the French and Indian War.

1763
The Treaty of Paris is signed on February 10 by England, France, and Spain, ending the French and Indian War.

1765
Parliament passes the Stamp Act on March 22. The Stamp Act Congress meets in New York City on October 17 to protest the tax; twenty-eight delegates from nine colonies attend. The act goes into effect November 1.

1767
Parliament passes the Townshend Act on June 29.

1770
In the Boston Massacre on March 5, British soldiers kill five colonists.

1773
Parliament passes the Tea Act on April 27; on December 16, during the Boston Tea Party, a group of men dressed as Native Americans board English ships and destroy cargoes of tea to protest the tax.

1774
Parliament passes the first of the Intolerable Acts on March 25; the First Continental Congress meets in Philadelphia on September 5; twelve colonies (all except Georgia) are represented.

1775

Parliament declares Massachusetts in a state of rebellion in February; Patrick Henry makes his famous declaration, "Give me liberty or give me death!" in Richmond, Virginia, on March 23; minutemen and the British clash at Lexington, Massachusetts, on April 19 to open fighting in the American Revolution; the Second Continental Congress convenes in Philadelphia on May 10; Congress names George Washington to head the Continental army on June 15; although the British drive Americans off Bunker Hill in Massachusetts on June 17, American troops fight bravely; on July 3 at Cambridge, Massachusetts, Washington assumes command of troops laying siege to Boston; on July 5 Congress adopts the Olive Branch petition, but Great Britain rejects it.

1776

Thomas Paine publishes *Common Sense* on January 9; from March 7 to March 17, the British evacuate Boston; Congress declares its independence from Great Britain on July 2; Congress adopts the Declaration of Independence, written by Thomas Jefferson, on July 4, but members do not sign it until August 2; in September Franklin is chosen by Congress to represent the United States in talks with France about aiding America in the war; on September 9 Congress resolves that the words *United States* will replace *United Colonies* to refer to America; during November and December, American forces retreat across the Delaware River from New York to New Jersey; on December 26 Washington captures nearly one thousand Hessian mercenaries in an early morning raid on Trenton, New Jersey.

1777

Washington again attacks in the early morning of January 3, winning a battle at Princeton, New Jersey; British defeat at Saratoga, New York, on October 17 is a major victory as 5,642 British and German troops surrender; on November 15 Congress adopts the Articles of Confederation at York, Pennsylvania; they are ratified in 1781; France recognizes U.S. independence on December 17.

1778

On February 6 France and the United States sign two treaties, one of alliance and one of amity and commerce, as France promises to aid America in its fight for independence; the British attack by sea in December and take Savannah, Georgia.

1779

U.S. and British troops skirmish around New York between May and September; John Paul Jones wins a major naval victory off the coast of England on September 23.

1781

Congress issues $191 million in paper currency, called Continentals, on January 1; the Articles of Confederation are ratified by the states in March; on September 28 American and French troops surround Yorktown, Virginia, and begin shelling the British; the British army, led by Lord Charles Cornwallis, surrenders at Yorktown, Virginia, on October 19; the surrender brings the war virtually to an end.

1782

On April 12 peace talks begin in Paris with Benjamin Franklin, the only U.S. representative; he is later joined by John Jay and John Adams; on June 20 Congress adopts the Great Seal of the United States; formal peace negotiations start in September; a preliminary peace treaty is signed on November 30.

1783

On September 3 America and Britain sign the Treaty of Paris, officially ending the war, while France and Spain sign separate treaties with England; the Continental army is disbanded on June 13; Washington resigns his commission as commander in chief on December 23.

1784

Congress ratifies the Treaty of Paris on January 14; in December Congress votes on plans for a permanent federal capital and designates New York as the temporary capital.

1785

On January 11 Congress moves to the newly designated capital, New York City; on May 20 Congress passes the Land Ordinance of 1784, dividing the Northwest Territory into townships.

1786

On August 7 a proposal is submitted to Congress to revise the Articles of Confederation; on September 11–14 delegates from New York, New Jersey, Delaware, Pennsylvania, and Virginia meet to consider commercial reforms; out of the Annapolis Convention comes the call for the Constitutional Convention.

1787

Constitutional Convention opens in Philadelphia on May 14 and delegates meet until September 17, when the Constitution is approved; every state except Rhode Island sends delegates; on October 27 the first of the *Federalist* papers appears in print; Delaware becomes the first state to ratify the Constitution on December 7.

1788

On June 21 New Hampshire becomes the ninth state to approve the Constitution, providing the two-thirds majority needed for ratification; Congress declares the Constitution to be in effect on July 2.

1789

On February 4 George Washington is elected president of the United States, John Adams vice president; the first session of the U.S. Congress begins on March 4; Adams is sworn in as vice president on April 21; on April 30 Washington is sworn in; Congress submits the proposed Bill of Rights to the states for ratification on September 25.

1790

On March 1 Congress authorizes the first U.S. Census; on May 29 Rhode Island ratifies the Constitution to become the thirteenth state; the census is completed on August 1 and shows a population of 3,929,625, including 697,624 slaves and 59,557 free blacks, with Virginia being the most populous state (747,610) and Philadelphia the largest city (42,444); on August 12 Philadelphia is designated the temporary capital.

1791

The Bank of the United States is chartered on February 25; on March 4 Vermont becomes the fourteenth state; Congress adopts the Bill of Rights on December 15.

1792

Congress passes the Coinage Act on April 1, authorizing the establishment of a U.S. mint and calling for a decimal system of coins and currency from dollars down to cents; on June 1 Kentucky, previously part of Virginia, becomes the fifteenth state.

1793

On March 4 Washington is inaugurated for his second term; on April 22 Washington issues a declaration of neutrality in the war between Great Britain and France, which began in February; Congress authorizes Washington, D.C., as the future capital of the United States on June 10.

1794

The U.S. Post Office is established on May 8; on November 19 special envoy John Jay and Great Britain sign the Jay Treaty to settle remaining differences between the countries following the Revolutionary War.

1795

On January 20 Congress passes the Naturalization Act, requiring residency for five years before citizenship can be granted.

1796

Tennessee becomes the sixteenth state on June 1.

1797

John Adams is inaugurated as the second president on March 4.

1798

Between June 18 and July 14, Congress passes the Alien and Sedition Acts.

1800

Washington, D.C., becomes the nation's capital in June; the first Congress to sit in Washington, D.C., convenes on November 17.

1801

On February 11 a tie in electoral votes between Thomas Jefferson and Aaron Burr is announced; on February 17, after thirty-six ballots, the House of Representatives elects Jefferson president and Burr vice president; on March 4 Thomas Jefferson is inaugurated as the third president.

1803

Ohio becomes the seventeenth state on March 1; between April 30 and May 2 the United States and France complete the Louisiana Purchase for $15 million, giving America another 820,000 square miles of territory.

1804

On May 14 the expedition of Meriwether Lewis and William Clark sets out from St. Louis up the Missouri River, reaching the Pacific Ocean on November 8, 1805; on July 11 Alexander Hamilton is fatally wounded in a pistol duel with Burr; on December 5, in the first election with separate voting for president and vice president, Thomas Jefferson is reelected.

FOR FURTHER READING

Robert C. Baron, ed., *Soul of America: Documenting Our Past, 1492–1974*. Golden, CO: Fulcrum, 1989. An excellent primary source for major documents and speeches that have been pivotal in U.S. history, providing the complete text as well as brief introductions that explain their importance.

Paul F. Boller Jr., *Presidential Anecdotes*. New York: Oxford University Press, 1981. A lighthearted look at presidents that shows their human side while detailing their major accomplishments.

James Daugherty, *Poor Richard*. New York: Viking, 1946. A biography of Ben Franklin entertainingly written for the younger reader.

Phillip T. Drotning, *Black Heroes in Our Nation's History: A Tribute to Those Who Helped Shape America*. New York: Cowles, 1969. An informative account of the role of African Americans in American history from the nation's founding through the civil rights battle.

Thomas Fleming, *Liberty! The American Revolution*. New York: Penguin, 1998. A thoroughly documented history of the Revolution, this book includes many large illustrations, many in color, and fascinating insights into what life was like during those years.

Winthrop D. Jordan, Miriam Greenblatt, and John S. Bowes, *The Americans: The History of a People and a Nation*. Evanston, IL: McDougal, Littell, 1985. A fact-filled basic history of America, focused on significant individual contributions.

Zachary Kent, *Encyclopedia of Presidents: George Washington*. Encyclopedia of Presidents Series. Chicago: Childrens Press, 1986. This biography for the younger reader contains essential facts about Washington's life and accomplishments.

Albert Marrin, *The War for Independence: The Story of the American Revolution*. New York: Atheneum, 1988. A detailed look at the war that won freedom for the United States. The author concentrates on the military aspects of the Revolution.

Ernest May, *A Proud Nation*. Evanston, IL: McDougal, Littell, 1984. An excellent textbook history of the United States.

Charles W. Meister, *The Founding Fathers*. Jefferson, NC: McFarland, 1987. This book offers brief sketches of the founders that contain interesting historical information and personal details.

Don Nardo, *Thomas Jefferson*. San Diego: Lucent Books, 1993. An excellent biography for the younger reader. The author uses a wide range of sources to present a balanced portrait of Jefferson.

Wendie C. Old, *George Washington.* Springfield, NJ: Enslow, 1997. A fact-filled biography for the younger reader.

Diane Ravitch, ed., *The American Reader: Words That Moved a Nation.* New York: HarperCollins, 1990. A collection of key documents in American history. An excellent sourcebook for students.

John F. Roche, *Illustrious Americans: Alexander Hamilton.* Morristown, NJ: Silver Burdett, 1967. An interesting biography that combines Hamilton's writings, including personal letters, with a detailed account of his life.

Jerry Silverman, *Songs and Stories from the American Revolution.* Brookfield, CT: Millbrook, 1994. This short, amusing but informative book features songs and stories of revolutionary times. It provides a unique glimpse into the minds and culture of early Americans.

Alfred Tamarin, ed., *Benjamin Franklin: An Autobiographical Portrait.* London: Macmillan, 1969. A collection of Franklin's writings: excerpts from letters, journals, pamphlets, and sections of his *Autobiography.*

David C. Whitney, *The American Presidents.* Garden City, NY: Doubleday, 1978. Short biographies that colorfully portray the presidents and explain their major accomplishments.

WORKS CONSULTED

Books

Bill Adler, ed., *The Kennedy Wit*. New York: Citadel, 1964. Examples of the humor that was so much a part of the charm of John F. Kennedy.

Catherine Drinker Bowen, *John Adams and the American Revolution*. Boston: Little, Brown, 1950. A detailed, personal look at Adams through the end of the Revolutionary War.

Fawn M. Brodie, *Thomas Jefferson: An Intimate History*. New York: W. W. Norton, 1974. The author researched thousands of letters that Jefferson wrote as well as his other works to provide a unique look at his personal life. The first to take an in-depth look at his controversial relationship with Sally Hemings.

Stuart Gerry Brown, *Thomas Jefferson*. New York: Washington Square, 1966. A comprehensive biography of Thomas Jefferson with quotes and facts from many different viewpoints.

Ronald W. Clark, *Benjamin Franklin: A Biography*. New York: Random House, 1983. An exhaustive biography that documents every significant event in Franklin's life and provides solid insights into his personality.

Margaret L. Coit, *The Life History of the United States*. Vol. 3. *1789–1829: The Growing Years*. New York: Time-Life Books, 1963. An informative, tightly written history of the period.

John A. Garraty with Robert A. McCaughey, *The American Nation: A History of the United States to 1877*. Vol. 1. 7th ed. New York: HarperCollins, 1991. The authors write authoritatively about American history, bringing it alive for the reader.

Richard D. Heffner, *A Documentary History of the United States*. Bloomington: Indiana University Press, 1952. Basic documents that are important to history, such as the Declaration of Independence and the Constitution.

Robert Maynard Hutchins, ed., *American State Papers: The Federalist*. Chicago: Encyclopaedia Brittanica, 1952. All of the essays that make up the *Federalist*.

Michael Kraus, *The United States to 1865*. Ann Arbor: University of Michigan Press, 1969. A scholarly look at the nation's early years, this work concentrates on why events took place rather than simply how they unfolded.

Richard B. Morris, *The Life History of the United States*. Vol. 2. *1775–1789: The Making of a Nation*. New York: Time-Life Books, 1963. An informative, tightly written history of the period.

———, *Seven Who Shaped Our Destiny: The Founding Fathers as Revolutionaries*. New York: Harper & Row, 1973. The author takes a critical look at America's founders, revealing their flaws and explaining how their personalities shaped their actions.

Willard Sterne Randall, *George Washington: A Life*. New York: Henry Holt, 1997. This exhaustive biography follows Washington's life in great detail, providing one of the most comprehensive portraits available of the first president.

Nathan Schachner, *Alexander Hamilton*. New York: D. Appleton-Century, 1946. A detailed, scholarly look at Hamilton's life.

Peter Shaw, *The Character of John Adams*. Chapel Hill: University of North Carolina Press, 1976. The author examines Adams in detail and portrays his personality, flaws and all.

Page Smith, *Jefferson: A Revealing Biography*. New York: American Heritage, 1976. An authoritative biography that probes the character and personality of Thomas Jefferson as well as his accomplishments.

———, *A New Age Now Begins: A People's History of the American Revolution*. 2 vols. New York: McGraw-Hill, 1976. Smith's two-volume history is one of the finest works ever written about the American Revolution. Also one of the most interesting, it employs a wide variety of sources to tell the story in human terms.

Periodicals

Eugene A. Foster et al., "Jefferson Fathered Slave's Last Child," *Nature*, November 1998.

Eric S. Lander and Joseph J. Ellis, "Founding Father," *Nature*, November 1998.

Internet Sources

National Archives and Records Administration, "The Declaration of Independence: A Transcription." www.nara.gov/exhall/charters/declaration/declaration.html.

INDEX

PICTURE CREDITS

Cover photos: (center) Library of Congress; (clockwise from top right) National Archives, Library of Congress, Library of Congress, National Archives

Archive Photos, 83

Archive Photos/American Stock, 32

Corbis/Bettmann, 91

John Grafton, *The American Revolution,* Dover Publications, Inc., 1975, 35, 36, 37, 47, 74

Library of Congress, 9, 17, 19, 22, 23, 24, 29, 39, 40, 42, 43, 49, 50, 51, 54, 58, 60, 65, 67, 69, 82, 95, 100, 106

National Archives, 76, 79, 87

North Wind Picture Archives, 64, 68

Prints Old & Rare, 12, 94, 99, 102

ABOUT THE AUTHOR

Michael V. Uschan has written seven books. His previous works include biographies of John F. Kennedy and Tiger Woods, *A Multicultural Portrait of World War I,* and *A Basic Guide to Luge,* part of a series written for the U.S. Olympic Committee. Mr. Uschan began his career as a writer and editor with United Press International, a wire service that provided news reports to newspapers and radio and television stations. Because journalism is sometimes called "history in a hurry," Mr. Uschan considers writing history books a natural extension of the skills he developed as a journalist. He and his wife, Barbara, live in Franklin, Wisconsin, a suburb of Milwaukee.